Common-Practice
Harmony

LONGMAN MUSIC SERIES

Series Editor: Gerald Warfield

Common-Practice Harmony

William H. Reynolds
University of California, Riverside

with
Gerald Warfield

LONGMAN
New York & London

Common-Practice Harmony

Longman Inc., 1560 Broadway, New York, N.Y. 10036
Associated companies, branches, and representatives
throughout the world.

Copyright © 1985 by Longman Inc.

Developmental Editor: Gordon T. R. Anderson
Editorial and Design Supervisor: Jennifer C. Barber
Production/Manufacturing: Ferne Y. Kawahara

Library of Congress Cataloging in Publication Data
Reynolds, William H., 1925–
    Common-practice harmony.
    (Longman music series)
    Includes index.
    1. Harmony.   I. Warfield, Gerald.   II. Title.
III. Series.
MT50.R4   1984   781.3   83-18707
ISBN 0-582-28426-0

Manufactured in the United States of America
9 8 7 6 5 4 3 2 1   93 92 91 90 89 88 87 86 85

Contents

Preface

This book has two goals: the first is to present, in a straightforward manner, those principles of harmony that are thought to be common to all tonal music; the second is to present for study specific musical compositions by composers of the eighteenth and nineteenth centuries. These compositions demonstrate the application of principles presented in the text, and their study will encourage the growth of a deeper understanding of tonal music.

Part writing (more specifically, *four*-part writing) is a method used almost universally to teach harmony, and it is also the method employed in this book. This is, of course, an important technique to learn; however, one should move through it without undue delay to additional musical studies that will put its creative and analytical principles to good use. To do so is important both because of the pressure of time in the undergraduate curriculum and because of the continuing growth and evolution taking place within the field of music. This book, then, presents a concise and disciplined approach that encourages rapid progress.

I have attempted to present basic principles clearly, avoiding wherever possible discussions of exceptions that can confuse beginning students. This text has been used successfully both in a one-year study of harmony and in a two-quarter course.

Part I provides a review of the basic information that students of harmony should already know. Students who lack this background should plan to spend more time on the first part than students who need only review this material; it should be thoroughly understood before students proceed to Part II.

Part II deals with the traditional principles of harmony. Although rules are presented, they are not arbitrary restrictions; they are intended to help students avoid problems. I have always encouraged students to test these rules by looking at actual music. Anyone can locate passages by recognized composers that do not "follow the rules," and students who can cite specific examples should be permitted to follow those examples.

Among the written exercises are a number of bass lines and soprano melodies that have been taken from music of the eighteenth and nineteenth centuries. These actual examples of music provide a more accurate style for the exercises and make them more musical.

Part III presents twenty short compositions, or sections of compositions, that can be used both as musical examples and as analysis assignments. They are intended to illustrate, in the context of the musical score rather than in fragmentary examples, how composers have used the material discussed in the individual chapters of Part II. Within the chapters, reference is made to portions of the examples of Part III that illustrate the principle being studied.

The music of Part III is also drawn from the eighteenth and nineteenth centuries. The individual pieces have been placed generally in chronological order to demonstrate some of the stylistic differences that exist in tonal music of different periods.

I have tried particularly in Part III to call attention to certain aspects of melodic description, partly to gain an understanding of good voice leading and partly to describe the function of melody in analysis. Of course, within the fabric of a composition, music involves progressions that are both linear and chordal. The awareness of how these aspects relate to one another in a unified musical whole is fundamental to the comprehension of music.

Finally, it is important not to think of harmony as a course in composing. It is, in fact, a course in the understanding of tonal music. Moreover, it is important to realize that music itself cannot be translated into words. It is a subtle language that speaks in its own terms. My hope is that this volume can give students an understanding of actual music, so that they will have less need to be dependent on harmony texts and other secondary sources.

Certainly I cannot conclude this preface without expressing my appreciation to several generations of students who tested earlier versions of this text while they were studying harmony. Moreover, I am deeply grateful to my colleague, Dr. Donald Johns, whose encouragement and constructive comments were of inestimable value. There were many others who contributed much to me in completing this work, and at the top of that list are Dr. Rosalie Schellhous, who offered many suggestions toward revision, and Gerald Warfield, with whom it has been a great pleasure to work.

William H. Reynolds

PART I

PREREQUISITES

CHAPTER 1

Notation and Pitch

The following skills are prerequisites for most harmony courses:

1. the ability to read notation;
2. an understanding of key signatures;
3. the ability to calculate intervals.

THE FIVE-LINE STAFF

Musical notation involves the use of an arrangement of five parallel lines called a staff:

Example 1

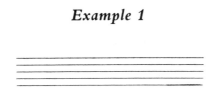

Both the lines and the spaces between the lines of the staff are used to indicate pitches. The higher a note is placed on a line or space of a staff, the higher the pitch, and, conversely, the lower the note is placed, the lower the pitch. Each staff requires the use of a symbol called the clef sign to assign specific pitches to the lines and spaces. Short lines (ledger lines) may be added above or below a staff to accommodate notes which exceed the limits of the staff.

CLEFS

Two clef signs are most frequently used: the treble clef 𝄞 and the bass clef 𝄢. When one of these is placed at the beginning of a five-line staff, it will indicate the specific pitch of each line or space in that staff. Two staves, one with a treble clef and one with a bass clef, combine to create a single notational structure called the grand staff. By using the treble and bass clefs in this manner, one can indicate the following pitches, all of which correspond to the following white notes on the piano keyboard:

Example 2

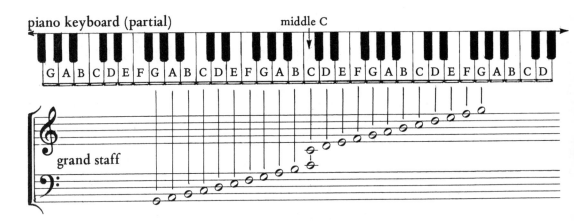

ACCIDENTALS (CHROMATIC ALTERATIONS)

In order to indicate the pitches that correspond to the black keys on the piano keyboard, it is necessary to employ a chromatic alteration (also called an accidental). The two accidentals in common use are the sharp (♯) and the flat (♭). A sharp placed to the left of a note head raises the pitch of the note to that of the next higher key (usually black) on the keyboard. For example, the note C on the treble staff, when preceded by a sharp, becomes C sharp; similarly, the note D can be altered to become D sharp.

Example 3

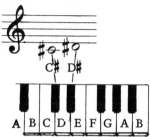

When a flat is placed to the left of a note head, the pitch is lowered to the pitch of the adjacent key (usually black) on the keyboard. For example, the note D can be altered to become D flat, and the note E can be altered to become E flat.

Example 4

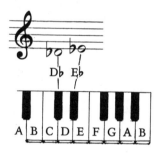

The use of sharps and flats makes it possible for keys on the piano keyboard to be indicated by two different pitch names. In the following illustration you can see that C sharp and D flat refer to the same key. Any two such note names are said to be enharmonic equivalents. D sharp and E flat are also enharmonic equivalents.

Example 5

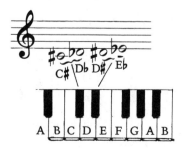

Note that the white keys of the piano keyboard make use of the first seven letters of the alphabet, repeated over and over again. Note also that the names of the white keys can be determined by their position in relationship to the black keys (which are grouped in twos and threes). The pitch C is always to the left of a group of two black keys, and the pitch F is always to the left of a group of three black keys.

Example 6

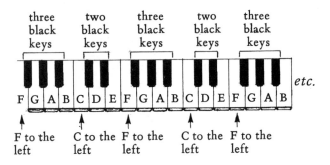

If it should become necessary to indicate that a previously altered note is to be unaltered (*not* sharped or flatted), a natural sign ♮ is used. This sign, when placed to the left of a note head, cancels an accidental that has been previously indicated.

WHOLE STEPS AND HALF STEPS

Two adjacent keys on a piano are a *half step* apart. Thus E and F are a half step apart. However, F and G, which have a black note (F sharp or G flat) between them, are a *whole step* apart. That is to say, two half steps equal one whole step. Similarly, F sharp and G are a half step apart, while F sharp and G sharp (with G in between) are a whole step apart.

Example 7

NOTE SYMBOLS AND REST SYMBOLS

The following are note symbols, with which you are familiar, and the rest symbols that correspond to each note value:

Example 8

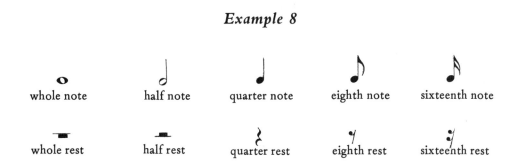

In placing note symbols on a staff, position the stems in the proper direction. In the context of a single melodic line, the note stems should point *up* if the note head is *below* the middle line of the staff. If the note head is *above* the middle line of the staff, the stem should point *down*. When the note head is *on* the middle line of the staff, the stem may point either up or down, to conform with the majority of the notes around it.

Example 9

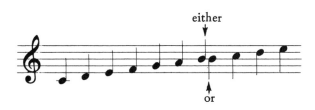

The exception to this rule (that note stems should point back into the staff) occurs when two different melodic lines are represented on the same staff. The most convenient way of differentiating between two melodic lines is for the stems of each line to point in opposite directions (that is, away from one another). This is the usual method for writing harmony exercises in which the soprano and alto lines will be written in the treble staff, and the tenor and bass lines will be written in the bass staff.

Example 10

soprano line
alto line

tenor line
bass line

In such cases, however, take care not to make the stems too long, so that they do not become confused with other notations on the staff.

EXERCISES

1. Place a treble clef sign on a five-line staff; then, on that treble staff, write quarter notes to indicate each of the following pitches. Do not add lines above or below the staff.

    E A C F D G B♭ F♯ G♯ C♯ D♯ G♭ E♭ A♭ D♭ E♯ C♭ F♭ B♯

2. Repeat exercise 1, this time using the bass clef.

3. Construct a grand staff. Using only the lines and spaces provided by that grand staff, plus an added line for middle C, write three different notes (at different octave levels) for each of the following pitches. Use whole notes.

    A E G B D F C A♭ E♭ G♭ F♯ G♯ C♯

4. Write the following notes as whole notes on a treble staff. Then, on another treble staff immediately below the first one, write one enharmonic equivalent for each note.

    B♭ E♭ A♭ D♭ C♭ F♭ F♯ C♯ G♯ D♯ E♯ B♯

5. Repeat exercise 4, this time using the bass clef.

Notation Workshop A

In Chapter 1 a number of music symbols were introduced. Chapter 2 presents the conventions for drawing such symbols by hand, that is, in manuscript form. It is important to follow notational conventions; otherwise, one's manuscript, even when correct in content, can have the appearance of musical illiteracy.

After reading each section of this chapter, examine your manuscript notation in light of the instructions given. How close are your clefs and notes to the way they should be drawn? Observe any differences and try to improve your manuscript technique. You may find it helpful to repeat the following exercises every two or three weeks throughout the semester until your manuscript has a professional appearance.

Exercises in this chapter follow the discussion pertaining to each exercise. There are five exercises in all.

THE TREBLE CLEF

An engraved treble clef looks like this 𝄞, and in manuscript it may be drawn like this 𝄞. Notice that the straight line with the crook at the end is slightly slanted to the left ⌡; that it protrudes above and below the staff about the distance of another line 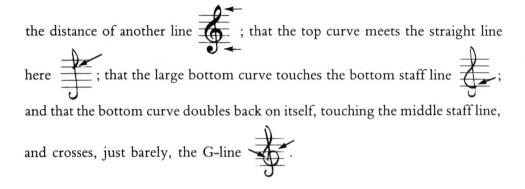 ; that the top curve meets the straight line

here 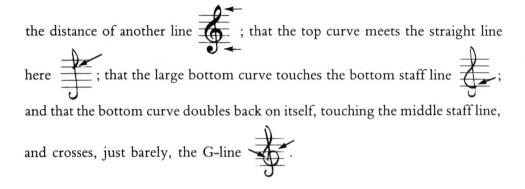 ; that the large bottom curve touches the bottom staff line 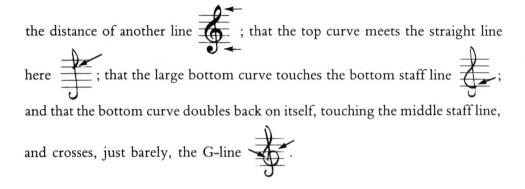 ;

and that the bottom curve doubles back on itself, touching the middle staff line,

and crosses, just barely, the G–line 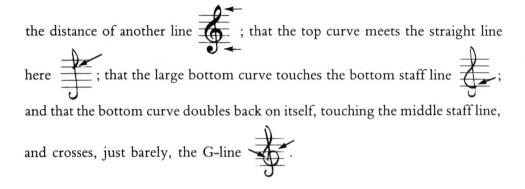 .

Exercise 1

On the top staff of a sheet of music paper, draw twenty slanted straight lines with hooks. Be careful not to slant them too much. Extend them above and below the staff about the distance of a space.

 *etc.*

Now add the rest of the treble–clef sign, starting at the top of the straight line. Check, in particular, the following points marked with arrows.

THE BASS CLEF

An engraved bass clef looks like this , and in manuscript it looks

very much the same . Notice that the small ball is on the F–line ;

that the tail of the sign goes into the bottom space ; and that the two dots

are on either side of the F–line .

Exercise 2

On the staff beneath exercise 1, draw twenty bass clefs. Be sure to "dot" each F-line as you go. Check the following points marked with arrows.

THE WHOLE NOTE

An engraved whole note looks like this **o**, and in manuscript it looks like this ⌒. Note that it is not round (in fact, *no* note heads are round). It is slightly oval and rests horizontally on or over a line

Exercise 3

On the staff below exercise 2, draw twenty whole notes. Place them on the second space from the bottom.

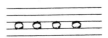

Check that they are slightly oval, that they rest horizontally, and that they are hollow (make sure your pencil is not so dull that the hollow space is filled in).

OTHER NOTE VALUES

The engraved half note and quarter note look like this ⟨image⟩, and in manuscript they are drawn ⟨image⟩. In this case, note that the heads of the notes, although oval, are at a slant.

When the stem of a note goes up it is placed on the right side of the note head, and when the stem goes down it is placed on the left side.

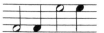

As mentioned in Chapter 1, in four-part harmony soprano and alto lines will be notated on the treble-clef staff, and tenor and bass lines will be notated on the bass-clef staff. Note the directions of the stems in the four-part example (see Chapter 1, Example 10).

When two voices on the same staff utilize the same pitch (for example, on the shared second note of the tenor and bass lines), the two stems are placed on the same note head.

However, this convention is not followed if there is any chance of confusion, for example, when one note is a half note and the other is a quarter.

The length of the stems, in four-part writing, should be about 2½ spaces long. If there is only one melody notated on the staff, then the stems are slightly longer (3½ spaces).

Notes in the space immediately above or below the staff should always touch the staff lines.

The size of the note head should comfortably fill one space (even if the note head is on a line).

Do not use a thin line for a note head or make the note head too fat.

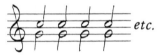

Exercise 4

On the staff below exercise 3, place a treble clef. Follow it with twenty half notes on C and twenty half notes on G, as shown.

 etc.

Make the slant of the half-note heads consistent, and do not make the stems too long.

Exercise 5

On the staff below exercise 4, place a bass clef. Follow it with twenty quarter notes on D and twenty quarter notes on F, as shown.

etc.

You will find that if you rotate the pencil very slightly after you make each note head, the pencil will make a thinner line for the stem.

CHAPTER 3

Scales and Keys

A *scale* is a collection of pitches arranged in ascending or descending order. The most common scales contain seven different pitches represented by the letter names A B C D E F and G (with or without chromatic alterations). It is usual to repeat the first pitch of the series at the end, making the scale a succession of eight pitches.

Example 1

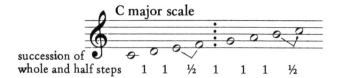

THE MAJOR SCALE

The scale in Example 1 is a C major scale for two reasons: It is a C scale because it begins and ends on C; and it is major because it contains the prescribed succession of whole steps and half steps that is found in any major scale. This succession creates the characteristic *sound* of the major scale with which we are so familiar. The study of harmony is primarily concerned with two types of scales—major scales and minor scales. Minor scales (to be considered later) have the same number of notes as major scales, but the prescribed succession of whole steps and half steps is different.

It is customary to assign Arabic numerals to each successive pitch of the scale and to refer to those successive pitches as first degree, second degree, third degree, etc. They are also known by the following names:

first degree—tonic   fifth degree—dominant
second degree—supertonic   sixth degree—submediant
third degree—mediant   seventh degree—leading tone
fourth degree—subdominant   eighth degree—tonic

TRANSPOSITION

Because there is an established succession of whole steps and half steps that identify the major scale, it is possible to shift that succession to any other position on the piano keyboard. That is, we can begin a major scale on any key of the piano keyboard so that the first degree of the scale (tonic) can be any white or black key. The only requirement in making such a shift is that we retain the same relationships between each of the degrees of the scale. This process is called transposition.

In order to keep the succession of whole steps and half steps that is prescribed for the major scale when we begin on any other pitch than C, it is necessary to make chromatic alterations to certain of the pitches. For example, if we wish to shift the major scale so that it can begin on D, we will have to use F sharp and C sharp in the scale:

Example 2

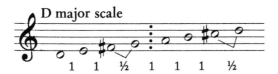

Likewise, the degrees of the scale shift so that, for instance, in D major, the second degree (supertonic) is E, the third degree (mediant) is F sharp, etc.

THE MINOR SCALE

The minor scale has three forms: natural minor scale, harmonic minor scale, and melodic minor scale.

Example 3

The natural minor scale (a minor)

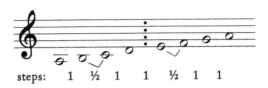

The scale in Example 3 is the natural form of the a minor scale for two reasons: It is an A scale because it begins and ends on A; it is the natural form of the minor scale because it contains the prescribed succession of whole steps and half steps that is found in natural minor scales.

The other two forms of the minor scale are:

Example 4

The harmonic minor scale (a minor)

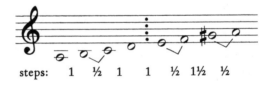

Example 5

The melodic minor scale (a minor)

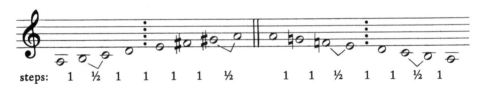

By comparing these two forms with the natural form we find that:

1. The harmonic form raises the seventh degree by a half step, creating a step and a half between the sixth and the seventh degrees.
2. The melodic form raises both the sixth and the seventh degrees by a half step as it ascends.

3. The descending form of the melodic minor scale is identical to the natural minor scale.

The alterations of the sixth and the seventh degrees in harmonic and melodic forms of the minor scale increase the tendency to move up to the tonic. This is done by the creation of a leading tone that is a half step away from the tonic. Because there is a whole step between the seventh and eighth degrees in the natural and descending melodic forms of the minor scale, there is not a strong leading tone emphasis in those forms.

All minor scales may be transposed in the same manner as has been explained for major scales. Again, the only requirement in making such a shift is that we retain the same relationships between each of the degrees of the scales.

Example 6

g minor (natural)

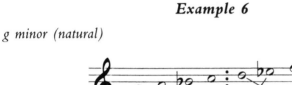

steps: 1   ½   1   1   ½   1   1

g minor (harmonic)

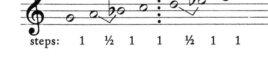

1   ½   1   1   ½   1½   ½

g minor (melodic)

steps: 1   ½   1   1   1   1   ½   1   1   ½   1   1   ½   1

Because we have not studied chords, it is not possible adequately to define *key* at this time. However, as a preliminary working definition, it is possible to state that a piece of music that principally makes use of the notes of a specific major or minor scale can be said to be in the key of that scale. In short, the tonic note of the scale indicates the key of the composition.

KEY SIGNATURES

Any major scale that does not begin on C and any minor scale that does not begin on A requires the use of chromatic alterations to retain the proper relationship among the notes of that scale. There is a convenient system for indicating the accidentals in such a situation. This system is called the *key signature*. The system is necessary because music in a specific key requires, as a matter of course, that specific notes be sharped or flatted throughout the piece. A key signature is simply a collection of the accidentals that normally appear in the scale of the key (with the exception of the variable sixth and seventh degrees of harmonic and melodic minor forms), and these accidentals are grouped together in a fixed pattern at the beginning of each line of music. Example 7 shows the major scale constructed on a tonic of A, and beside it, the same scale using the key signature of A major. Example 7 also shows the g minor scale and its key signature.

Example 7

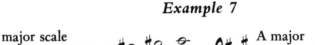

The order in which the accidentals appear within a key signature is important. Flats and sharps appear in a specified order and in certain regular positions on the staff.

Example 8

Flats: B E A D G C F   *Sharps:* F C G D A E B

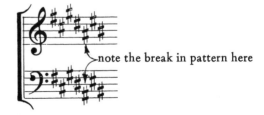

note the break in pattern here

Note that the order of sharps is the reverse order of flats.

HOW TO READ A MAJOR KEY SIGNATURE

1. For flat key signatures, the tonic is the line or space on which the next-to-last flat is found.[1]
2. For sharp key signatures, the tonic is the line or space a half step above the last sharp.

Examine the key signatures in Example 9 to verify these rules:

Example 9

F   Bb   Eb   Ab   Db   Gb   Cb   G   D   A   E   B   F#   C#

HOW TO CONSTRUCT MAJOR KEY SIGNATURES

1. Using the series B E A D G C F for flats and the reverse, F C G D A E B, for sharps, determine how many sharps or flats to use.
   a. *Flat Keys:* Counting from left to right in the series, go one letter past the tonic; this will show how many flats to place on the staff.
   b. *Sharp Keys:* Determine which pitch letter is the leading tone of the key and count from left to right in the sharp series until you come to that letter; this will show you how many sharps to place on the staff.
2. Place the required number of flats or sharps on the staff, following exactly the order and pattern shown in Example 9.

MINOR KEY SIGNATURES

For every major key there is a minor key that makes use of the same key signature. The minor key is known as the *relative minor* of the major key that has the same signature. Conversely, the major key having the same signature as

1. The key of F has only one flat and is the only flat key that does not have a flatted note as a tonic.

a minor key is known as the *relative major*. Thus major and minor keys having the same signatures are relative to each other. The key of C major has the same key signature as a minor (no sharps or flats). The key of a minor is thus the relative of C major, and C major is the relative of a minor.

Be sure to remember that all minor key signatures produce the natural form of the minor scale. The chromatic alterations that produce the melodic or harmonic forms of the minor scale can never be included in a key signature.

RULE FOR MINOR KEYS

1. The tonic of the minor key is located three half steps down from the tonic of its relative major key. Thus, *the tonic of the minor key is the submediant of its relative major.*

2. To construct a minor key signature, count up three half steps[2] from the minor tonic to locate the tonic of the relative major. Write that key signature. Thus, *the tonic of the relative major is the mediant of the minor scale.* *Note:* If the tonic of the relative major is on a line, the tonic of the relative minor will also be on a line; or, if the tonic of one is on a space, the tonic of the other will also be on a space.

Example 10

PARALLEL KEYS

Major keys and minor keys that have the same tonic are said to be parallel keys. For example, the parallel minor of C major is c minor. Parallel keys, not being relative to each other, have different key signatures.

Example 11

2. Using three different letter names, including the starting and ending notes.

CHROMATIC SCALE

If one should take a major scale and fill in every pitch between the two tonics (the first and the eighth degrees of the scale), the result would be a scale of twelve different pitches, each of which is separated from its adjacent pitch by a half step. This scale is called a chromatic scale. If one should build such a scale in the context of C major, or for that matter in the absence of any key, its ascending form would introduce the additional notes by using sharps, and its descending form would introduce the additional notes by using flats.

Example 12

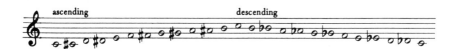

However, in a musical passage the chromatic scale will usually appear within a context governed by a key signature. When a key signature is used, the natural sign must also be used to cancel the effect of preexisting accidentals. In constructing a chromatic scale in the context of a key that uses sharps or flats in the signature, the function of the scale will become clear if the major scale of the key is written first (as shown by the whole notes of Example 13). The next step is to fill in every possible half step (where whole steps appear in the original scale) by using accidentals that *raise the original scale degrees ascending* and *lower the original scale degrees descending*. Example 13 is an illustration of the chromatic scale in the context of E flat major. Note that the fourth note is F sharp, not G flat, and that the fourth note from the end is G flat, not F sharp.

Example 13

Example 13 contains two kinds of notation that we have not used before. The first (C flat) is an accidental indicating a white key on the keyboard. There are four white keys that can be indicated in this manner:

Example 14

The second is the use of a double flat (♭♭). There is also a symbol for a double sharp (✗), an entirely new sign not shown in the example. Such double accidentals alter the indicated note by *two* half steps; B double flat thus indicates a pitch identical to that of the note A.

EXERCISES

1.   Write out the following major scales. Do not use key signatures. Insert appropriate accidentals to retain the necessary whole-step and half-step successions.
     a.   In the treble clef, ascending only:
          F major
          E♭ major
          D♭ major
          G major
          A major
          B major
     b.   In the bass clef, ascending only:
          B♭ major
          A♭ major
          D major
          E major
          F♯ major

2.   Write out the following minor scales. Do not use key signatures. Insert the appropriate accidentals to retain the necessary whole-step and half-step successions.
     a.   Natural minor scale in the treble clef, ascending only:
          d minor
          f minor
          e minor
          c sharp minor
     b.   Harmonic minor scale in the bass clef, ascending only:
          g minor
          b flat minor
          b minor
          g sharp minor

    c. Melodic minor scale in the treble clef, both ascending and descending:
      c minor
      e flat minor
      f sharp minor
      d sharp minor

3. Notate, on a grand staff, the following major key signatures:

B	C	D flat
E	F	G flat
A	B flat	C flat
D	E flat	F sharp
G	A flat	C sharp

4. Notate, on a grand staff, the following minor key signatures:

b	c	d sharp
e	f	g sharp
a	b flat	c sharp
d	e flat	f sharp
g	a flat	a sharp

5. Notate chromatic scales in both ascending and descending forms in each of the keys indicated. Use key signatures. Follow the form of Example 13 by using white (whole) notes for pitches that are within the key and by using black notes for pitches that are not in the key.
    a. In the treble clef:
      E flat major
      A major
      c minor
      f sharp minor
    b. In the bass clef:
      B major
      D flat major
      g minor
      b minor

6. Here are the begnnings of five melodies. No key signatures are used; instead, each accidental is marked. Answer these questions for each melody.
    a. List the notes, in ascending-scale order, that are found in the melody.
    b. Based on the notes that do appear, in what key is the melody? If there are two possibilities, give both.
    c. Based on your answer for both a and b, what notes do not appear in the melody?

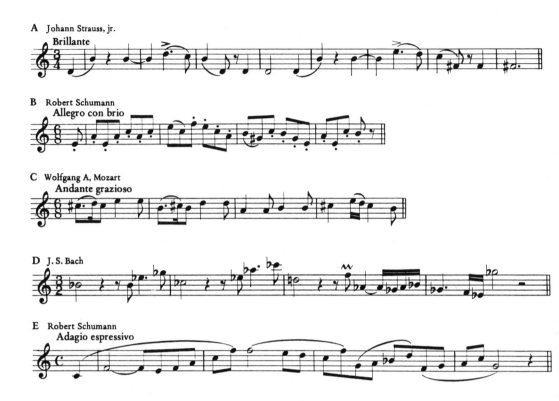

CHAPTER 4

Intervals and Triads

INTERVALS

An interval is the distance between two tones. It is calculated by counting all of the lines and spaces between the two tones, *including the lines or spaces on which the two tones are written.* The interval is identified by this procedure in terms of its numerical value.

Example 1

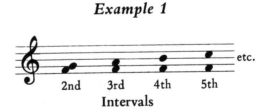

2nd   3rd   4th   5th

Intervals

Two notes occupying the same pitch form the interval of a unison; numbers from 2 to 7 are expressed as ordinal numbers (second, third, fourth, etc.); and the number 8 is expressed as an octave. Any interval with a numerical value greater than an octave is a compound interval. For example, a tenth may also be called a compound third (in which case it is regarded in the same manner as a third). An eleventh may be called a compound fourth, etc. Intervals are melodic if their two tones are sounded consecutively and harmonic if they are sounded together.

Example 2

melodic intervals   harmonic intervals

5th   7th   3rd   6th   6th   3rd   5th   8ve

However, numbers alone are not specific enough to identify intervals, since there can be several "sizes" for each number. For example, the first melodic fifth interval (Example 2) could have been from G up to D natural instead of to D sharp. It is necessary, in addition to numerical specifications, to have qualitative terms specifying the different sizes that can occur for each numerical category. The terms that indicate the quality of intervals are perfect, major, minor, augmented, and diminished.

RULE FOR CALCULATING THE QUALITY OF AN INTERVAL

1. Consider the lower note of an interval to be the tonic; if the upper note of the interval is found in the major scale of which the lower note is the tonic, the interval is either perfect or major. Perfect intervals are unisons, fourths, fifths, and octaves. Major intervals are seconds, thirds, sixths, and sevenths.

2. If the interval is a half step greater than either a perfect interval or a major interval, then it is augmented. If it is a half step smaller than a major interval, it is minor. If it is a half step smaller than either a perfect interval or a minor interval, it is diminished.

The following chart illustrates the rule stated above:

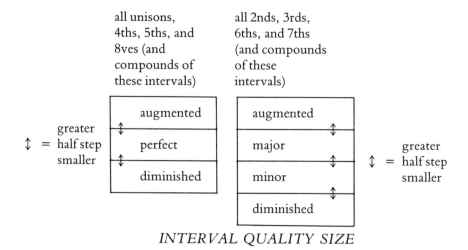

INTERVAL QUALITY SIZE

In the chart, each classification may be changed to the one above or below by increasing or decreasing the specific interval by a half step. But note that it is impossible to change a perfect interval into a major interval or a minor interval. Similarly, it is not possible to change a major interval or a minor interval into a perfect interval.

For analytical convenience the following abbreviations are used to designate the quality of an interval:

augmented ... A
perfect   ... P
major   ... M
minor   ... m
diminished ... d

Complete interval specification requires first the designation of the quality and then the designation of the quantity of an interval, as shown in Example 3.

Example 3

ENHARMONICS

Enharmonic notes are notes that have different spellings, but have the same pitch sound. The spelling of a pitch has to do with its meaning (function), and the meaning of a pitch becomes clear when that pitch appears in a musical context. In our use of language we have a similar circumstance when words like "see," "sea," and "C" sound the same, but obviously have different meanings. Example 4 shows a variety of enharmonic spellings of notes that have the same pitch sounds.

Example 4

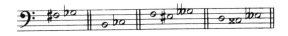

Two enharmonically equivalent intervals will indicate the same keys on the piano keyboard, but two different intervallic functions are actually involved. Again, the functions of these intervals can only become apparent in a musical context. Example 5 shows a few enharmonically equivalent intervals.

Example 5

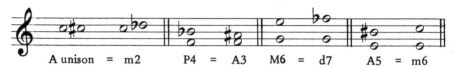

A unison = m2   P4 = A3   M6 = d7   A5 = m6

Note: The first enharmonic interval, C to C♯, is an augmented unison, not a second.

One occasionally encounters intervals that, by means of chromatic alteration, are increased beyond the dimensions of an augmented interval or are decreased under the dimensions of a diminished interval. When such is the case, the interval is called doubly augmented or doubly diminished.

Example 6

dbly. A4   dbly. d8   dbly. d5

The rules for calculating the numerical value and quality of intervals have already been stated. However, it is possible to make additional observations at this time that may be helpful both in identifying intervals and in constructing them. In any case, these observations can provide an additional point of view by which one can verify interval calculations.

1. All fourths and fifths on the unaltered (no accidentals) musical staff are perfect, except those that involve the notes F and B sounding together.
2. Minor seconds are made up of 1 half step; major seconds are made up of 2 half steps; minor thirds are made up of 3 half steps; major thirds are made up of 4 half steps.
3. Major sevenths are 1 half step smaller than an octave; minor sevenths are 2 half steps smaller than an octave; major sixths are 3 half steps smaller than an octave; minor sixths are 4 half steps smaller than an octave.

TRIADS

A triad is a combination of three tones that, when placed in the closest possible relationship to each other, result in a structure of two superposed intervals of a third. The lowest of the three tones is called the *root* of the triad; the tone a third above the root is called the *third*; and the tone a fifth above the root is called the *fifth*.

Example 7

Triads may be built on any degree of the scale. It is customary to identify them in musical analysis by using the Roman numeral corresponding to the scale degree (of the key) on which the root of the triad occurs. Thus, if the root of the triad is on the tonic note of the scale, the triad is identified by the Roman numeral I; if the root of the triad is on the subdominant note of the scale, the triad is identified by the Roman numeral IV. Example 8 illustrates triads built on every degree of the C major scale. The intervals by which the triads can be identified are also shown.

Example 8

It is apparent that some of the triads are built from the same intervals. The following list shows which triads share interval structure and which are different:

Triads	Intervals	Kind
I, IV, & V .... contain	.....P5 & M3.....	major triad
II, III, & VI ... contain	.....P5 & m3.....	minor triad
VII......... contains	.....d5 & m3.....	diminished triad

Example 9 shows triads built on every degree of the *harmonic*[1] form of the c minor scale. Again, the intervals by which the triads can be identified are shown.

---

1. If the *natural* form of the minor scale were shown, III and VII would both contain a P5 and M3 (as major triads), and V would contain a P5 and m3 (as a minor triad).

Example 9

The following list groups the triads of the c minor scale in accordance with their interval qualities.

Triads		Intervals		Kind
V & VI	contain	P5 & M3		major triad
I & IV	contain	P5 & m3		minor triad
II & VII	contain	d5 & m3		diminished triad
III	contains	A5 & M3		augmented triad

From the groupings shown, four kinds of triads emerge, each with a distinctively different sound:

Major: major 3rd and perfect 5th above the root
Minor: minor 3rd and perfect 5th above the root
Diminished: minor 3rd and diminished 5th above the root
Augmented: major 3rd and augmented 5th above the root

Example 10

major triad   minor triad   augmented triad   diminished triad

Note: In Example 9, using the harmonic form of the minor scale, it was possible to demonstrate all four kinds of triads. However, in actual music, the augmented triad on III occurs only rarely. Instead, the seventh degree of the scale is unaltered (following the form of the *natural* minor) so that III usually is found in minor keys as a major triad.

Example 11

c: augmented III
is rare.

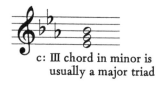

c: III chord in minor is
usually a major triad

ROOT POSITION AND INVERSIONS

Triads occur in a variety of positions in musical contexts, so that the root, the third, and the fifth may be arranged in many ways. For pedagogical reasons, we will begin our study of harmony by only constructing triads with the root in the bass. At the appropriate time we shall introduce triads with other notes of the triad in the bass.

1. When the *root* of the triad is in the lowest voice, the triad is in *root position* (regardless of the arrangement of the other notes of the triad above it).
2. When the *third* of the triad is in the lowest voice, the triad is in *first inversion* (regardless of the arrangement of the other notes of the triad above it).
3. When the *fifth* of the triad is in the lowest voice, the triad is in *second inversion* (regardless of the arrangement of the other notes of the triad above it).

Example 12

root position   first inversion   second inversion

VOICING

The study of harmony usually involves part writing—that is, writing for four parts. Normal vocal ranges for each part should be employed because the music will be primarily in a chorale style. The soprano and alto parts should be placed together on the treble staff, and the tenor and bass parts should be placed together on the bass staff. In most instances the voice ranges shown in Example 13 should not be exceeded.

Example 13

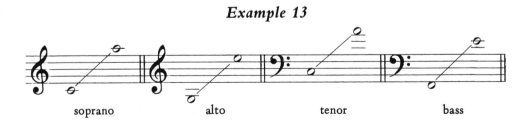

soprano   alto   tenor   bass

Since a triad consists of only three tones, one of the three tones must be doubled when we create a four-part harmonization. For the present, while the use of triads is limited to root position, the most satisfactory note to double is the root. Until we take up the study of doubling in a later chapter, the rule is: *Always double the root.*

SPACING

Following three suggestions concerning the distance between adjacent voices (spacing) will avoid many problems:

1. Do not exceed the interval of an octave between soprano and alto, or between alto and tenor.
2. The octave may be exceeded between tenor and bass.
3. Obtain variety in spacing by alternating use of *open* and *close* position (discussed below and shown in Example 14).

In *close position* the three upper voices, each on a different chord tone, occupy less than the interval of an octave. (Thus the distance between the tenor and the soprano will be less than one octave.) There is no possibility of inserting another chord tone between any of the three upper voices.

In *open position* the three upper voices occupy a space greater than an octave. There is an empty line or space on which an additional chord tone could be placed between the soprano and alto, or between the alto and tenor. (But remember, there must not be more than an octave between any two adjacent voices except the tenor and bass.)

Example 14

close   open   close   close   open   open   close   open   open   open

EXERCISES

1. a. Construct the following *melodic* intervals above the note D, bass clef:

    P5, m3, A8, d4, M10, m6, A6, m2, dbly.d8, d5

    b.   Construct the following *harmonic* intervals below the note C sharp, treble clef:

           m7, A6, d3, P4, m9, A2, dbly.A5, M3, m10, d8

2.   Write enharmonic intervals for each of the following intervals, varying only the upper note. Label each. In some cases more than one answer will be possible.

M3 _____ P8 _____ M2 _____ m3 _____ m7 _____ P4 _____ M6 _____ A3 _____ A6 _____ A4 _____

3.   Construct triads (three notes only) on each degree of the scale for the following keys; identify each triad by Roman numeral; and state whether the triad is major, minor, augmented, or diminished. Use whole notes.

        Major (use treble clef): G, F, B flat, D, A, E flat, E
        Harmonic minor (bass clef): e, a, d, b, g, c sharp, f
        Natural minor (treble clef): c, f sharp

4.   In four parts on the grand staff, construct all of the triads that occur in the following keys; indicate the Roman numeral; and identify the kind of triad in each case. Use whole notes.

        Major: B, E, A flat, D flat
        Harmonic minor: b flat, e flat, c, f
        Natural minor: a, g, f sharp

5.   In four parts on the grand staff, doubling the root in each case, construct three different open and three different close positions of the following triads. Use whole notes.
    a.   V in c sharp minor (harmonic form)
    b.   III in a minor (natural form)
    c.   II in B major
    d.   VI in g minor (harmonic form)
    e.   IV in e minor (harmonic form)

6.   Transpose the following triads down a major third, still using four parts on the grand staff. Indicate whether each is major, minor, augmented, or diminished.

7. Locate the root of each of the following triads, and indicate the appropriate Roman numeral for each. State whether each is major, minor, augmented, or diminished. *Note:* The root may not be in the bass of these chords.

CHAPTER 5

Meter and Rhythm

Rhythm is the pattern, in time, that is articulated by the notes of a composition. However, it is the duration (rather than the pitch) of those notes that is the important component of rhythm. For example, one could take a pencil and tap on a desk the way "Dixie" goes:

Example 1

The pitches of "Dixie" obviously are not present, but the rhythm is.

Meter is the regular pulse that serves as a framework, or background, to rhythm.

When a marching band is marching just to drums, the patterns played by the drums (assuming more than a simple boom every time one puts one's foot down) are an example of rhythm. The footsteps of the band members are a manifestation of meter.

Rhythm and meter, although closely related, are easily distinguished from one another. In the band example, the band will continue to step (manifestating the meter) whether or not there is a note played (articulating the rhythm) on every step. Certainly, the band does not take a step only when a note is played (that is, step to the rhythm). That would make for a very humorous effect, indeed.

The band could also perform the march in concert. The individual notes of the march would still articulate the rhythm, but there would be no marching to mark the meter. The conductor, however, would be signaling the meter to the band (along with the tempo) through his conducting. Even without the conductor, the musicians and listeners would still "feel" the regular meter of the piece while they heard the rhythms. In fact, it is essential for listeners to feel the meter in order to hear a piece in a coherent manner.

One might ask if the meter is the same thing as the beat. It is not. A regular beat may be present throughout a piece, but it is not, by itself, the meter. The meter is the *organization* of the beats into patterns of strong and weak beats. This is true even for the marching band example because in marching there is slightly more emphasis placed on the left foot and the beat to which that corresponds. The regular *left*-right-*left*-right transforms regular beats into a hierarchy of strong, weak, strong, weak; and this organization of the beats is meter.

The meter is partly reflected in musical notation by the measure; that is, by vertical lines (barlines) that divide the five-line staff into spatial measures, each graphically representing an equal passage of time. Each measure will contain the same number of two, three, four, or more, beats.

Example 2

measures of a staff marked off by barlines

The simplest meters can be either felt as duple or triple, with recurring patterns of |>−|>−|>−| for duple (this is the meter of a march) and patterns of |>−−|>−−| for triple (this is the meter of a waltz). Another simple meter is quadruple; it involves patterns of |>−>−|>−>−|. As the stresses for quadruple meter show, it is very much like a double duple meter; and it is often difficult, when listening to music, to distinguish between duple and quadruple. Notice that the strongest pulse is always on the first beat. In quadruple, there is also a slight accent on the third beat.

METRIC SIGNATURES

Composers specify the meter of music by indicating a metric signature at the beginning of a piece or a section of a longer composition. Metric signatures are two numerals, one above the other, in which the lower numeral indicates the kind of basic note value employed (half note, quarter note, etc.) and the upper numeral indicates the number of these notes required to fill a single measure. Thus the total durational value of the time signature appears within each measure.

There are two types of metric signatures: simple and compound:

$\dfrac{2}{2}$ $\dfrac{2}{4}$ $\dfrac{2}{8}$——duple (2 beats to a measure)

$\dfrac{3}{2}$ $\dfrac{3}{4}$ $\dfrac{3}{8}$——triple (3 beats to a measure)

$\dfrac{4}{2}$ $\dfrac{4}{4}$ $\dfrac{4}{8}$——quadruple (4 beats to a measure)

Simple Meters

In simple meters the note values may subdivide into smaller values by a ratio of 2:1.

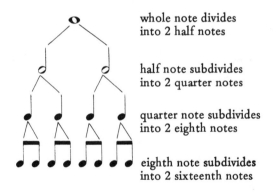

whole note divides
into 2 half notes

half note subdivides
into 2 quarter notes

quarter note subdivides
into 2 eighth notes

eighth note subdivides
into 2 sixteenth notes

Subdivision of Note Values in Simple Meter

The possibility of dividing note values by a ratio of 3:1 also exists. When this is specified by means of the metric signature, the meter is compound.

$\dfrac{6}{2}$ $\dfrac{6}{4}$ $\dfrac{6}{8}$——compound duple (2 beats to a measure)

$\dfrac{9}{4}$ $\dfrac{9}{8}$——compound triple (3 beats to a measure)

$\dfrac{12}{4}$ $\dfrac{12}{8}$——compound quadruple (4 beats to a measure)

Compound Meters

In compound meter each beat has specified for it a subdivision consisting of three notes.

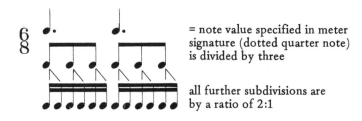

= note value specified in meter signature (dotted quarter note) is divided by three

all further subdivisions are by a ratio of 2:1

Example of Subdivision in Compound Meter

Compound meters can be perceived in two different ways, depending on whether the tempo is fast or slow. For example, the most common compound meter, $\frac{6}{8}$, can be heard as duple at a fast tempo (two dotted quarters per measure), or sextuple (double triple) at a slow tempo, with six eighth notes per measure (although the listener will still hear an emphasis on the first and fourth eighth notes). Similarly, a group of nine notes can seem like three groups of three at a fast tempo, and a group of twelve can seem like four groups of three.

	six	nine	twelve
fast:	>−	>−−	>−>−
slow:	>−−>−−	>−−>−−>−−	>−−>−−>−−>−−

Two Ways to Perceive Compound Meters

TYPES OF RHYTHM

In the music appropriate to the study of harmony, the tendency to form rhythmic patterns by repetition is a frequent means of achieving musical coherence. The following melody, from Example Eleven (in Part III), will illustrate such repetition.

Example 3

repeated rhythmic patterns

Melodic rhythm (as in Example 3) is concerned with durational patterns that occur in melodic lines. When the full musical context is included with this melody, one can see that Beethoven provided contrasting rhythms in the chordal accompaniment of the left hand. Moreover, the second–beat dynamic accents further complicate the rhythmic scheme by disguising the metric patterns normally encountered in $\frac{4}{4}$ meters.

Example 4

Harmonic rhythm, is formed by the durations, not of specific tones, but of chords—and can be defined as rhythm that is created by the frequency of chord change. The following examples (in Example 5) show two contrasting kinds of harmonic rhythm.

Example 5

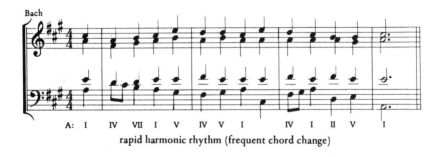

rapid harmonic rhythm (frequent chord change)

slow harmonic rhythm (few changes of chord)

Tonal music consists of melodic rhythm and harmonic rhythm interacting with one another and with the metric structure. There are also other rhythms formed by dynamic contrasts or even melodic contours. In subsequent discussions of form and repetition of patterns, as well as in the discussion of phrases and cadences, we will encounter the interaction of rhythm with other aspects of music. The following examples (in Example 6) show that sometimes the rhythms of melody, harmony, and meter may coincide in a simple manner with each other; or, as is usual, these rhythmic factors may be independent of each other, involving complex interrelationships.

Example 6

EXERCISES

1. a. On music manuscript paper, placing all of the notes on the middle line of the staff, in the manner of Example 1, write out (measure by measure) the melodic rhythm of the highest instrumental part of these examples from Part III:

    Example Five (J. Strauss, Waltz from "Blue Danube")
    Example Nine (Haydn, Andante from Quartet in F, op. 74)
    Example Fourteen (Schumann, "Träumerei")

    b. Then, in the space below the staff, write out (measure by measure) the metric patterns that continue throughout each of the three examples in a. Use the symbol > to indicate accented beats and the symbol − to indicate unaccented beats.

2. Determine the appropriate meter for each of the following rhythmic examples, then draw in the appropriate barlines. Add the necessary upper numeral to complete the metric signature for each line. In every case, the basic unit of the beat will be a quarter note. If there is a pickup to the first measure, the value of that note will be subtracted from the notes in the last measure. (Such pickups occur in exercises e and f.) Note that no duration may be held over a barline without a tie.

3. Write out rhythmic notation appropriate to the following poetic texts, as though you were setting them to music. First, determine which syllables are accented and which are unaccented; then, choose a metric signature that enables those syllables to be appropriately accented or unaccented. That meter will continue throughout the poem. There is no single "correct" setting, as the following different versions of the first line of the first poem will show:

a. But ere we this perform,
    We'll conjure for a storm
    To mar their hunting sport,
    And drive them back to court!

Nahum Tate, 17th c.

b. Sweet Nymph, come to thy lover!
    Lo, here alone our loves we may discover;
    Where the sweet nightingale with wanton glozes,
    Hark, her love too, discloses.

                        Unknown, 16th c.

c. O, hush thee, my baby, thy Sire is a knight,
    Thy mother a lady, both lovely and bright;
    The woods and the glens from the tower which we see,
    They all are belonging, dear baby, to thee.

                        Sir Walter Scott, 18th c.

CHAPTER 6

Notation
Workshop B

At this point you will have utilized a large number of music notation symbols in doing the exercises of Chapter 5. In the present chapter we will introduce the notational conventions appropriate to some of those symbols, in particular, some that were not covered in Chapter 2. Compare these symbols with the way you constructed them earlier and try to improve your notation accordingly. You may wish to repeat the exercises in this chapter several times in the course of the semester, until your notation has a professional appearance.

As in Chapter 2, the exercises follow the discussion that pertains to them. There are six exercises in all.

ACCIDENTALS

Sharps

The sharp is the most difficult of the accidentals to draw properly. First of all, it is *not* square, like a tic-tac-toe grid.

incorrect

The sharp consists of two thin vertical lines, the right one slightly higher than the left one,

and two thick slanted lines that cross the vertical lines. The thick horizontal lines are slightly shorter than the vertical ones.

By varying the degree with which you press down on the pencil, and by rotating the pencil slightly, you can make a graphically correct manuscript sharp.

The second important feature of the sharp is that it is, in fact, larger than it is usually drawn. The total height of a sharp should be about three spaces.

3 spaces high

correct height of sharp

Exercise 1

On the first staff of a manuscript page of music paper place a treble clef. Then, write out twenty third-space C sharps (quarter-note C's with a sharp in front). Do not make the sharp square. Do use thin vertical lines that are slightly staggered ( ); do make the cross-lines thicker; and do make the sharp three spaces high.

Flats

The flat is slightly smaller than the sharp; the total height is about two and a half spaces.

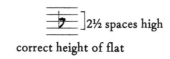

2½ spaces high

correct height of flat

Also, the rounded part of the flat should be slightly larger than a space.

slightly larger than 1 space

correct size for body of flat

Exercise 2

On the second staff of your manuscript page, beneath exercise 1, place a bass clef. Then write twenty second-line B flats aligned beneath the C sharps on the first staff. Do not make the flats too small.

Naturals

Like the sharp, the natural sign is not square either. The cross-lines are slightly slanted and, also like the sharp, they are thicker than the vertical lines. The total height of the natural is three spaces.

] 3 spaces high

correctly drawn natural

Exercise 3

On the staff below exercise 2 place a treble clef. Write twenty second-line G naturals (quarter-note G's with a natural in front) aligned with the B flats on the second staff. Do not make the natural too small.

METRIC SIGNATURES (TIME SIGNATURES)

The metric signature appears immediately after the key signature.

The two numbers of the metric signature should be clear, appear within the staff, and be divided by the middle line of the staff. Do not draw a line between the numbers such as is used for fractions. When indicating a metric signature in a printed context, do not write it as a fraction (that is, with a dividing line). The numbers should properly only appear above one another: $\frac{4}{4}$, not $\frac{4}{4}$. Metric signatures, after appearing on all first-measure staffs, are not repeated on subsequent or continuation staff lines. They are assumed to remain in effect for the duration of the piece or movement unless changed by the appearance of a new metric signature.

FLAGS

The eighth-note flag should extend to the level of the note head.

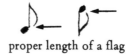

proper length of a flag

Note that the flag is on the right side of the stem no matter whether the stem points up or down.

Be careful not to make the flag too short or to leave it "waving."

flag too short   flag not close enough to stem

For sixteenth notes, the second flag is added inside the first. Also, note that the two flags touch at their tip.

sixteenth-note flags touch at their tips

Exercise 4

On the staff below exercise 3 draw a treble clef. Notate twenty eighth-notes on the top-line F. Do not make the flags too short.

Exercise 5

On the staff below exercise 4, draw a bass clef. Notate twenty eighth-notes on the top-line A. Check that the flags are not too open (left "waving").

Exercise 6

On the staff below exercise 5, draw a treble clef. Notate twenty sixteenth–notes on the second-line G. Make sure the two flags touch at their tips.

BEAMS

Beams are flags that connect two notes;  is the same as ♪♪. The most important aspect of beaming is that only notes within the same beat should be joined together. This helps the performer to grasp the meter and the rhythmic patterns more quickly. For instance $\frac{3}{4}$ ♪♫♫♪♪ is clearer and easier to perform than $\frac{3}{4}$ ♪♫♪ ♪. Such beaming can be particularly helpful in compound time.

Notes of different values may be beamed together if they are in the same beat , and observe that the sixteenth beam on the final note of the last example is *under* the joining beam (that is, not extending out on the right side).

Sometimes, in $\frac{4}{4}$ time, notes of the first and second beats, and notes of the third and fourth beats, are beamed together. However, this happens only when there are four eighth notes to join, thus keeping the major metric structure of the measure clear.

PART II

PRINCIPLES OF HARMONY

CHAPTER 7

Harmonic Progression: Basics

When a triad, in a four-part context, moves to another triad, it can do so only by means of the movement of its individual parts; in other words, each soprano, alto, tenor, and bass part must literally move from one note to another (or, it may hold over or repeat the same note). This movement—a melodic process—is called voice leading. Although the present chapter is about harmonic progression (the connection of triads one with another), this process cannot be understood properly without first discussing the movement of the individual parts, the voice leading.

VOICE LEADING

It is theoretically possible to connect any two triads if clear and unambiguous melodic movement has been used in each of the parts. The vertical sounds of four such melodies working together are harmonies and harmonic progressions. The melodies producing these harmonies must be responsive to the sense of overall harmonic progress that serves the needs of the music; however, the concern at this point is that we learn to control the voice leading so that it is melodically clear, and so that the resulting harmonies involve suitable chord progressions. Keep the following rule in mind: *When connecting one chord to another, move each voice part as little as possible; thus, move each voice part to the nearest available note of the next chord.*

This rule does not imply that it is musically or artistically more satisfying to move by step than by leap; however, when one is beginning to write harmonic progressions, the melodies will be easier to control if stepwise movement is used.

Example 1

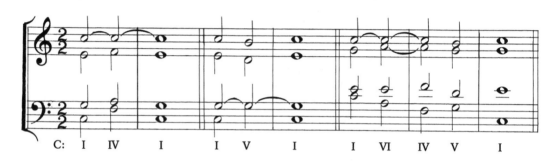

C: I IV I   I V I   I VI IV V I

The examples shown in Example 1 are not formulas for composing. Their intent is to demonstrate the clarity of part writing. One should bear in mind that a leap, particularly in an inner voice, is liable to cause confusion between melodic lines; however, if stepwise motion is used, such confusion is much less likely to occur. Adjacent voices should not cross above or below one another.

Example 2

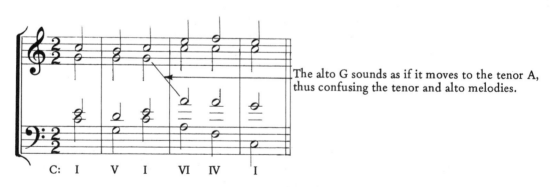

C: I V I VI IV I

The alto G sounds as if it moves to the tenor A, thus confusing the tenor and alto melodies.

More will be said about melodic writing in Chapter 8.

BASIC HARMONIC RELATIONSHIPS

If we look again at key signatures, we will find that keys share the most pitches with each other when their tonics are a perfect fifth apart. For example, the key of C has six pitches in common with the key of G and six pitches in common with the key of F. Those keys with many pitches in common with each other are thought to be closer to one another than those keys with few pitches in common.

The arrangement of key signatures in the so-called circle of fifths (see Example 3) shows that the tonics of closely related keys, moving one way around the circle, bear the relationship of tonic to dominant. Moving the other way around the circle, the relationship of closely related tonics is that of tonic to subdominant.

Example 3

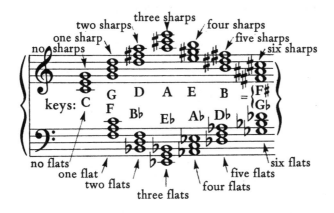

Circle of Fifths

The triads built on I and IV and V (in any key) are often called *primary triads*. This is largely because these harmonies function in a tonally unambiguous way to create a sense of key feeling. In fact, IV and V are the only triads within a key that normally lead directly to I in the formation of a cadence[1] (the final two chords of a phrase or the final two chords of a composition).

---

1. See Chapter 9.

Example 4

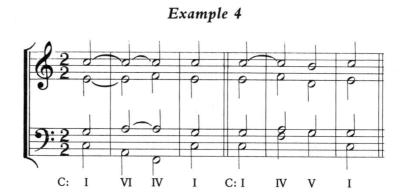

Their importance in cadences does not mean that these triads necessarily occur with greater frequency than other triads; in fact, in some contexts one may find II used more frequently than IV. It merely means that IV and V, having such a direct relationship to I, provide a great deal of tonal emphasis. In fact, the greatest tonal emphasis in tonal music is provided by the progression V–I, and it also provides the greatest feeling of finality. In a sense, all other harmonies bear a supportive role to the dominant-tonic relationship. Nevertheless, the choice of one chord instead of another depends primarily on the ease with which the individual voices can move from one chord to the next. Another consideration is the suitability of the second chord in terms of harmonic function and sound quality. With these points in mind, it may be helpful now to consider some of the similarities and differences that triads and progressions exhibit.

The *tonic triad* (I) is the primary chord of the key and is nearly always the last chord of any piece. It appears throughout a composition and often moves to IV or V, but can move with ease to any other triad in the key.

The *dominant triad* (V) seeks vigorously to move to I (its leading tone seeks to resolve to the tonic note). When it does resolve to I, it establishes or asserts a feeling of the key, particularly when it does so at the end of a phrase. It may move frequently to VI, and sometimes to III. Movement to other chords should be treated with care.

The *subdominant triad* (IV) moves most often to V or to I. It can also move to II. When it moves to V it is usually participating in a progression that strongly emphasizes the key, because the V will usually proceed on to I.

The *supertonic triad* (II) moves most often to V and also to VI. Occasionally it moves to III. When it moves to V it is usually participating in a progression that defines the key; that is, the V will usually proceed on to I, thus presenting two successive progressions with dominant-to-tonic root relationships, moving around the circle of fifths.

The *submediant triad* (VI) shares two pitches with the I triad. It can function as a relief from I since in major it is a minor triad and in minor it is a major triad. It moves easily to II or IV, and sometimes to III.

The mediant triad (III) is used less frequently than the other chords. It is considered to be close to the I triad because it shares two pitches with I and because its root is a member of the I chord. Like VI it can be used to provide relief from I because in a major key it is minor and in a minor key it is major. It moves easily to VI or IV, and sometimes to VII.

The leading-tone triad (VII) functions as a substitute for V.

ROOT MOVEMENT

Triads whose roots are a fourth or a fifth apart have only a single note in common with each other. Thus, a progression involving movement between such triads provides a considerable newness of sound, presenting five of the seven notes of the scale; but, at the same time, the common tone between the two triads provides a kind of harmonic link by carrying over a portion of the sound from one chord to the next. Root progressions by a fourth or a fifth are probably the most frequent of all progressions: I–V, V–I, I–IV, IV–I, II–VI, VI–II, VI–III, III–VI.

Example 5

Triads whose roots are a third apart can be thought of as relatives of one another. The fact that there are two tones in common between triads whose roots are a third apart (as in I and III), so that only one new note is introduced, causes the triads in these progressions to sound somewhat similar to each other. The same is true of V and III, and of IV and II.

Progressions in which the root movement is *down* a third (as opposed to up a third) are successful because the tone not in common (between the two triads) is the root of the second triad. The most influential tone of a triad, from a standpoint of overall sound, is its root. Thus the movement of a root up a third (to a strong note already present) may not sound like much of a change of chord. The following progressions occur frequently: I–VI, VI–IV, IV–II, V–III, I–III.

Example 6

Note that I–III is the only example of root movement up a third.

C: I VI VI IV IV II V III I III

Triads whose roots are a second apart have no notes in common, but they do have a stepwise relationship between each of the three tones of the triads. This kind of progression combines much new sound with the possibility of good voice leading through stepwise movement. Progressions in which the root is moving up a step are quite common, and they can generally be expected to produce a satisfactory sense of harmonic movement. However, the reverse (root movement down a second) is much less often used. Most common are IV–V and V–VI; other possibilities include I–II, II–III, and III–IV.

Example 7

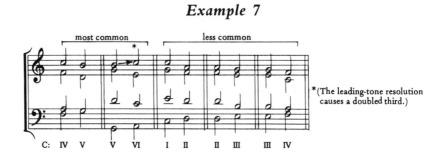

most common   less common

*(The leading-tone resolution causes a doubled third.)

C: IV V   V VI   I II   II III   III IV

SUMMARY OF STRONG PROGRESSIONS

Strong progressions are progressions that composers of tonal music have used with the greatest frequency. They are also, as a rule, unambiguous with respect to the key in which they function; therefore, they are often employed at structurally significant places in the music. Although for the time being all assignments in this book will specify the chords to be used, the following summary of strong progressions is offered to help in the development of a sensitivity to those progressions that can be most successfully employed. It is a guide only and is not intended to replace the composer's ear in deciding the suitability of a given progression.

Strong progressions: Root movement up or down a fourth or a fifth.
Root movement up a second.
Root movement down a third.

RULES FOR CONNECTING TRIADS

These rules are not arbitrarily imposed restrictions, but are intended to help students to learn to write clear and unambiguous progressions. They will also help to prevent the most common part-writing errors. *For the time being these rules do not apply to the bass* since we are restricted to root movement (that is, the bass line simply moves mechanically from root to root).

1. Move each voice part as little as possible; this is to say, move each voice part to the nearest available note of the next chord. (The result will be a soprano that is more static than is desirable; however, the following chapters will gradually encourage an intelligent use of greater freedom.)
2. Hold over any common tones between adjacent triads, except in the progression II–V in minor keys.
3. Always resolve the leading tone of a dominant chord. The leading tone regularly resolves up by half step to its tonic; also, where appropriate, it may be held over as a common tone with the next triad. (The following chapters will introduce certain exceptions to this rule.)
4. Generally move the soprano in the opposite direction of the bass. Fewer problems will be encountered if this rule is followed. It is not possible, however, to use this kind of writing exclusively.
5. Avoid any dissonant (augmented or diminished) melodic intervals.
6. Avoid moving from one perfect fifth to another perfect fifth between any two voices; avoid moving from one perfect octave to another perfect octave between any two voices. *Simply stated:* Avoid any parallel perfect fifths or parallel perfect octaves (or unisons) between any two voice parts.

Example 8

a. Common tone is held over as is expected in the progression I–IV.

C: I   IV

b. There are two common tones in the progression I–VI and both are held over.

C: I   VI

c. The progression V–I involves the correct resolution of the leading tone (B to C).

C: V   I

d. The leading tone (B) has been held over, a perfectly acceptable treatment since the leading tone is a member of both chords.

C: V   III

e. The leading-tone tendency has been frustrated by leaping from B to E instead of resolving to C as expected. This is not acceptable treatment of the leading tone.

C: V   I

f. The augmented second in the soprano is an error caused by holding over the common tone in II–V in minor keys (the exception to the rule to hold over).

g. The correct treatment of II–V in minor (with doubled root) is bass up, other voices down.

h. The progression IV–V, incorrectly written, results in parallel fifths and parallel octaves.

i. The corrected IV–V progression shows that the bass moves up and the other voices move down.

The guidelines outlined in this chapter are intended to introduce the process of writing progressions. The kind of writing that can be managed at this stage falls far short of genuinely musical examples, but it is a beginning point on which more musical exercises can subsequently be built.

AVOIDING PROBLEMS—RULES OF THUMB

There are three specific progressions that present unique problems. The following rules of thumb are offered so that such problems as were shown in items f and h of Example 8 can be avoided.

1. In the progression IV–V (and in other progressions involving root movement up a second) move the bass up and the other three voices down.
2. In the progression V–VI, move the bass and the leading tone up and the other two voices down. (The resulting chord of VI will have a doubled third degree, but this is correct in this progression.)
3. In the progression II–V *in minor keys only*, move the bass up and the other three voices down.

Example 9

a. Bass up, other three voices down.

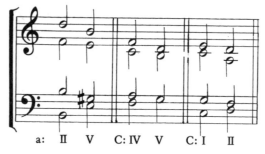

a: II   V   C: IV   V   C: I   II

b. Bass and leading tone up, other two voices down.

C: V   VI   C: V   VI

(Note that in the progression V–VI, the resolution of the leading-tone B results in a doubled third in VI.)

EXERCISES

Note: Write all four-part assignments, unless otherwise instructed, on the grand staff: SA, treble clef; TB, bass clef. Use only root-position triads unless otherwise instructed.

1. a. Starting in open position, using whole notes without barlines, make a four-part harmonization of the following:

    G: I IV I V I VI IV I

    b. In the key of d minor, make a four-part harmonization of the progression in 1–a above.

2. Make a four-part harmonization of the following root progression:

    a: I IV V I II V I V VI IV V I

3. Make a four-part harmonization, using only root progressions, of each of the following bass lines. Follow carefully the rules for connecting triads described in this chapter.

4. The following harmonization contains many errors; locate as many of these as possible. Copy the example as it is, then circle or otherwise mark the incorrect note or motion. Label each error.

5. Make a harmonic analysis (supply Roman numerals for each chord) of Example One ("Old Hundredth"), which is found in Part III of this book. As you will see, five of the chords in Example One are not in root position. Identify those chords and indicate which tone (third or fifth) is in the bass. Examine also the soprano melody and mark with brackets any similar melodic patterns that may occur in the soprano melody.

CHAPTER 8

Harmonic Progression: Techniques

In the discussion of voice leading with which we began the previous chapter, two points were made: (1) chords change by means of moving from one melodic note to the next in each of the four parts (soprano, alto, tenor, bass); and (2) stepwise movement within each melody is an unambiguous means by which a clear sense of melodic movement is achieved. Obviously, the use of stepwise movement alone can create a static and boring melody. The use of leaps is also an important factor in creating a good melody. However, it is desirable, in using leaps, not to rupture the sense of continuity or progress that is basic to the melodic line or to cause the lines to become confused with one another.

In Example 1 we can see that, between the stepwise melodic notes and between the notes that are leaping, a different kind of relationship exists. Leaps often imply a chord since they frequently are used to outline a triad. In such a case, the chord is being expressed horizontally as a melody, rather than vertically. As a result, the melody is infused with clear harmonic implications. Note that the first eleven notes of the melody in Example 1 are all members of the C major triad.

Example 1

underlying structure consisting of stepwise motion

In actual music, melodies commonly are more elaborate versions of a basic melodic line. For example, a melody may prove to be the elaboration of a single stepwise line:

Example 2

melody

basic line of that melody

Or, more than one basic line may be presented:

melody

basic lines of that melody

All musicians need to develop a sensitivity to the basic melodic lines that underly such musical passages as those shown in Example 2. The creation of a good line, even in an inner voice of a harmonization, will almost always be more important than any rule of harmony. In the next chapter, dealing with phrases and cadences, we will see that both melodic movement and harmonic progressions have a sense of direction that ultimately leads to a point of articulation (somewhat analogous to punctuation in language) called the cadence. Good melodies and good harmonic progressions are engaged in the creation of tension or suspense, leading to a point of arrival involved with a relaxation of that tension or suspense. Thus, even now we should become aware that melodies and harmonies do not merely fill out space in time, but need to embody a sense of movement and direction.

FREER VOICE LEADING

The rules that were given in Chapter 7 and the exercises at the end of that chapter do not permit the creation of melodic lines that are musically very interesting. As this study of harmony progresses, we will introduce techniques and procedures that can make the exercises more musical. Certain practices are offered in the examples below that begin gradually to approach greater freedom and complexity.

1. When one is harmonizing a bass line in which a chord is held, repeated, or sustained, direction or a sense of motion can be provided by simply changing the position of the other voices.

Example 3

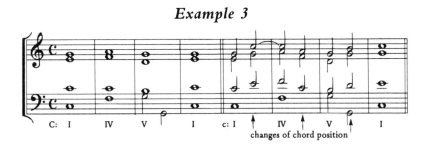

2. It is often helpful to change from closed to open position in order to avoid crowding the voices too closely, particularly when a descending soprano line or an ascending bass line begins to restrict freedom of movement.

Example 4

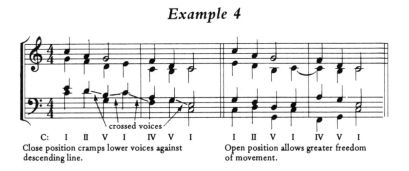

3. The occasional use of three roots and a third, particularly in the triads of I, IV, and V, may offer a helpful solution to many voice-leading problems, or may free a given voice for a better melodic contour. Where three roots and a third are used in four-part writing, the fifth of the triad is the degree commonly omitted.

Example 5

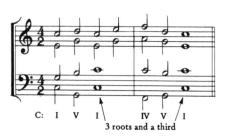

4. Often an increase in variety may be obtained by not holding over a common tone between adjacent triads, thereby freeing that voice so that it may move to another note. But this technique should be used with caution, because holding over common tones is both good voice leading and a means of avoiding certain voice-leading problems.

Example 6

5. In an inner voice, the resolution of a leading tone may successfully be taken over by an upper voice in order to allow the part containing the leading tone to move downward by step or by leap of a third (a frequent circumstance in final cadences). In Example 7, the leading-tone resolution is taken over by the voice immediately above the voice containing the leading tone.

Example 7

6. As shown in Example 8, a good melodic line may justify the nonresolution of the leading tone. Such cases are acceptable exceptions to the principle of always resolving leading tones, but should only be used when there is no other satisfactory choice.

Example 8

7. Any doubling may be justified (even doubling two leading tones) if good meldoic lines exist in both parts and the parts are moving in contrary motion. Again, this practice should be followed only when there is no other satisfactory choice.

IMPLEMENTATION

The following harmonic progression (Example 9) is presented in three different versions in order to illustrate the different problems one can encounter either in a very strict (unmusically so) setting or in the freer settings made possible by using some of the suggestions in this chapter.

Example 9

Strict and simple setting—correct, but unmusical

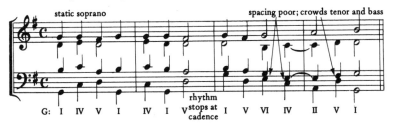

First freer setting

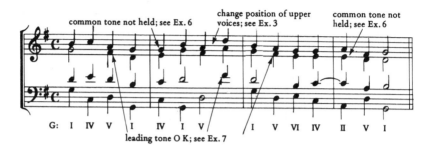

Second freer setting

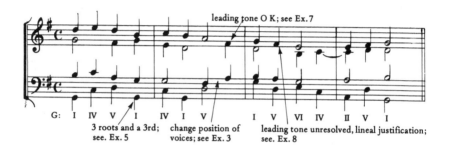

PROBLEM PROGRESSIONS

It is important to apply these suggestions for freer voice leading both cautiously and sparingly. With the use of freedom may come greater musicality; however, as the level of complexity increases, the opportunity to make mistakes also increases.

Parallel Octaves and Parallel Fifths

These intervals are formed (as we learned in Chapter 7) when two voices that are a perfect fifth (or a perfect octave) apart move to another perfect fifth (or another perfect octave), still involving the same two voices. In other words, the voice parts are moving with exactly the same interval in exactly parallel motion. We know that composers have strictly avoided such motion in tonal music. In addition to this kind of voice-leading problem, an additional problem—the direct octave and the direct fifth—should now be introduced.

Direct Octaves and Direct Fifths

These intervals are formed when two voices move from any interval by similar (not parallel) motion to a perfect fifth or a perfect octave. In certain cases there is no objection to such movement, but there are circumstances in which composers have generally avoided direct octaves and direct fifths. The following rule is offered as a simple guide.

RULE FOR DIRECT OCTAVES AND FIFTHS

Do not approach the interval of a perfect octave or a perfect fifth from the same direction between outer voices, unless the soprano is moving by step.

Example 10

a.   Incorrect: perfect fifth between outer voices approached by leap, same direction, both parts; perfect between outer voices, approached by similar motion, soprano not moving by step.

b.   Correct: soprano moving by step.

Note: Example 10a and 10b involve two different progressions. If it were necessary to preserve the melodic line in Example 10 a, the other voices would have to be changed.

Progressions Involving the Diminished Fifth

Progressions involving the perfect fifth moving to a diminished fifth are always acceptable. Progressions involving the diminshed fifth moving to a perfect fifth are acceptable only when the diminished fifth is not formed with the bass. This is different from the rule for direct fifths because, even if the soprano moves by step, the progression is incorrect when the diminished fifth is between the bass and one of the upper voices.

Example 11

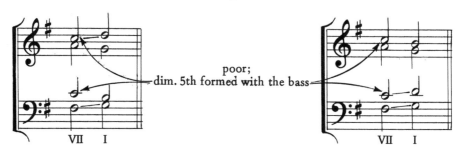

poor;
dim. 5th formed with the bass

VII   I   VII   I

DOUBLING AS A MEANS OF EMPHASIZING TONALITY

One of the more limiting aspects of the voice-leading rules we have used up to this point is that requiring root doubling. Any examination of actual music will reveal that other notes in a triad are doubled as well. Although doubling should be the result of good voice leading, there is also a purely tonal emphasis that can result from doubling. In other words, we will now consider the effect that doubling has on key emphasis. An important function of any harmonization is to make use of sufficient variety in the selection of chords. At the same time, it is important to reinforce the feeling of a key center in order to avoid any undesired feeling of vagueness or tonal ambiguity. Until now, we have simply doubled the root of root-position triads. By choosing to double pitches that are important in the overall key, more flexibility in doubling can be introduced.

Tonal and Modal Degrees

In comparing the major scale of any key with its corresponding parallel (not relative) harmonic minor form, it is apparent that certain notes remain unchanged between the two scales, while certain other notes differ. The unchanged notes are 1, 2, 4, 5, and 7; those that differ are 3 and 6.[1]

---

1.   The raised leading tone is so important in the dominant triad that the harmonic minor form is a basic scale in the study of harmony. Because descending melodies may follow the natural minor form, the seventh degree does not *always* appear as a leading tone.

Example 12

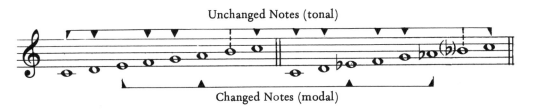

Unchanged Notes (tonal)

Changed Notes (modal)

The tonal function of the unchanged notes in the two scales shown in Example 12 is to present a general feeling of C. One cannot determine from those notes whether the scale is C major or c minor. Thus, if one chooses to double the notes C, D, F, or G (1, 2, 4, 5), the feeling of C will be reinforced, without specifying which (major or minor) scale of C is involved. Note that the seventh degree ought not to be doubled, because it is a leading tone. For purposes of doubling, then, we shall call 1, 2, 4, and 5 *tonal degrees*.

The distinction between the major or minor form of the scale can only be made by using those scale degrees that *do* change between the two forms, 3 and 6 (and 7 if the natural minor scale is used). Accordingly, 3 and 6 (and sometimes 7) are called *modal degrees*.

Tonal degrees: 1, 2, 4, and 5
Modal degrees: 3, 6 (and 7 in natural minor)

Tonal doubling is a process by which we can expand our options in choosing notes to double, and the rules for doubling can now be revised accordingly.

RULES FOR DOUBLING

1. In root position it is customary to double the root unless an awkward voice-leading situation is created.
2. It is acceptable to double a tonal degree, regardless of whether or not it is a root.[2]
3. Only for good melodic purposes should modal degrees be doubled.

Example 13 shows all the triads of the key of C major, with the root, third, or fifth of the triad doubled in each case. Triads that are unmarked have a doubled tonal degree; bracketed triads have a doubled modal degree; and triads that have been crossed out have a doubled leading tone. *Note:* The last triad in the series is VII, in which the fifth of the triad has been doubled; although the note

2. Remember that the progression V–VI involves doubling the third of VI. This is an instance of tonal doubling.

is F (a tonal degree), it is a poor note to double because one should not double any degree that forms a dissonant interval with another note of the triad. F–B (a diminished fifth) is a dissonant interval in the triad of VII.

Example 13

| M. D. = modal doubling | M.D. | | M.D. | doubled L.T. | | M.D. | doubled L.T. | | doubled L.T. | doubled dim. 5th |

EXERCISES

1. Harmonize the following bass lines in four parts, using root progressions. Make two versions of each, beginning the second with a different positioning of the voices. For instance, if close spacing was used the first time, try a more open positioning of voices next. In the second version, try to make a more satisfactory soprano melody than was possible in the first version. You may find that some of the suggestions for freer voice leading discussed in this chapter may assist you in making a more interesting soprano.

2. The following harmonization contains many errors; locate and identify as many of these as possible. First add chord symbols; then circle the wrong note or otherwise indicate any incorrect motion.

3. Following the guidelines provided by the *Summary of Strong Progressions* in Chapter 7, make up two different root-progression bass lines of your own (do not write out the upper voices). These should be about four measures in length; use duple meter for one and triple meter for the other. One should be in a major key, and the other should be in a minor key. Begin each with the progression I–VI, and end each with the progression V–I. Change chords on every successive beat.

4. Make a four-part harmonization of each of the root-progression bass lines you have constructed in exercise 3. You may alter the original version of the bass line if you feel there was something unsatisfactory at some point in the original version.

CHAPTER 9

Phrases
and
Cadences

PHRASES

The musical phrase is a complex structure of melodic, harmonic, and rhythmic components. It is a brief portion of a musical composition that has a beginning, a middle, and an end. It can be described as providing a short period of motion followed by a moment of pause or a point of arrival. A piece of music is made up of many phrases that follow one another in continuous succession. Although phrases may vary in length, the most common phrases within a piece of music from the eighteenth and much of the nineteenth centuries are generally of uniform duration, normally either two or four measures in length. The points of arrival ending phrases represent greater or lesser degrees of pause or repose. The greatest relaxation comes at the end of the final phrase of a piece, when the music comes to a complete stop. The point of pause or point of arrival that ends the phrase is called a *cadence*.

Singers and those who play wind instruments can physically experience *melodic* phrases in a most natural way because, when they need to breathe, it is logical for them to breathe between phrases. The melodic phrase is sometimes pictorialized in musical editions by an arch drawn from the beginning of a phrase to the end of it (see Example Sixteen, Part III). In historical editions of chorale settings (see Examples One and Two, Part III), fermata signs were customarily used to indicate the last note or chord of a phrase (functioning as signals to breathe, rather than as indications to prolong). Anyone who performs adequately as a musician must be aware of the phrase divisions that occur in a piece of music.

The rhythm associated with the melodic phrase is so essential to the nature of the melody that familiar pieces may be easily recognized merely by tapping the rhythms of that melody. But other rhythmic factors participate in the life of the musical phrase. One of these is the metric pulse, which determines the musical measure, and the other is the rhythm of the harmony.

HARMONIC RHYTHM

Chord changes usually occur with a certain amount of regularity; thus, it is possible to examine a piece of tonal music to determine its basic harmonic rhythm (the regular frequency with which chord changes take place).

In the discussion about chord progressions in Chapter 7, several points were made about chords and harmonic progressions:

1. A change of chord should involve a certain amount of newness of sound (diversity through the introduction of new notes).
2. However, a change of chord should provide an opportunity for smoothness as well (unity through good voice leading).
3. Some progressions involve a sense of drive, as in the progression V–I (which defines the key center with clarity).
4. Some chords, like III and VI, add color to the harmonic vocabulary and are less effective in defining the key center.

CHORD CHANGE AND METRIC ACCENT

Just as we learned in Chapter 5 that the meter of music sets up patterns of pulses involving strong and weak beats, we can now realize that changes of chord provide a structural analogy to metric accents. The strongest accent within any measure occurs on the first beat of the measure; the weakest accent of the measure occurs on the last beat. In other words, the strongest rhythmic area (from the standpoint of metric accent) occurs as the barline is crossed. It is the normal pattern for a change of chord to coincide with the first beat of the measure, thereby coordinating metric accent and harmonic strength.

A great deal of music involves a change of chord across every barline, and much music has a change of chord on almost every metric pulse. The first two examples in Part III of this book illustrate that kind of writing (which is common in the four-part choral style with which we will be occupied). Other styles, such as ballad style, or the dance style of the Strauss waltz (Example Five, Part III), may involve less frequent changes of chord. It will simplify matters at this point if we assume that crossing a barline will usually require a change of chord. By this process the harmonic rhythm will be coordinated with the metric rhythm.

HARMONY AND THE STRUCTURE OF THE PHRASE

The musical phrase was described at the beginning of this chapter as having a beginning, a middle, and an end. We have already discussed the fact that the final chord of any piece is normally going to be I, and we have found that I is usually preceded in cadences by V, or occasionally by IV. I, IV, and V have been called primary triads and are such strong indicators of the key center that it is safe to use them anywhere within the musical phrase. The triads of II, III, and VI provide an easy ambience within the harmonic vocabulary that introduces color, but does not necessarily indicate the key. In fact, III and VI are the triads that determine the modality (scale), not the key. Because of this ambient quality, II, III, and VI are often used within a phrase to provide contrast with the strong tonal implications of the primary triads. Thus, they are a practical means of enabling the phrase, somewhere in its midsection, to digress from the tonal strength of the beginning and the end of the phrase. Often a V–VI or a V–III progression is a means of propelling the phrase away from I, so that a more circuitous approach may be made to the cadence.

The beginning of the phrase often reinforces the key, particularly if it is the first phrase of a piece or the beginning of a new section of music. One would not begin a piece, as a rule, with the triads of II, III, or VI. While these triads may occasionally be used to begin some internal phrases, II and III are quite unsuitable for use as the final chord of a phrase. The triad of VI can be used as the final chord of a phrase if a deceptive cadence is involved. This will be explained in the following section.

CADENCES

Cadences can be described as similar in function to such punctuation marks as the comma or the period. They may suspend the forward motion of a piece of music for an instant, or they may bring the music to a complete stop. Cadences are the closing progression of any and all phrases in tonal music, and as a result they clarify the overall structure of a composition. Just as there are different kinds of punctuation marks signifying different kinds of pauses in speech, there are also different kinds of cadences in music. The main types are *authentic, half, deceptive,* and *plagal.*

Authentic

V–I. An authentic cadence is a full stop, much like a period in speech. There are two kinds:

Perfect authentic: Root-progression V–I, with the tonic note in the soprano of I. This is the most final of all cadences.

Example 1

Imperfect authentic: Any V–I cadence that departs from the requirements of a perfect authentic cadence: for example, if either V or I (or both) should be inverted; or if the third or the fifth of the tonic triad is in the soprano. Although this cadence is final in feeling, it is less likely than the perfect authentic cadence to stand at the end of a piece.

Example 2

Half

I–V, II–V, IV–V, etc. A half cadence occurs when a phrase ends on V. In this case a partial stop occurs, much like a comma in speech. Occasionally phrases may also end on IV, and these may be seen to function as half cadences unless they are preceded by V (discussed in the following paragraph).

Example 3

Deceptive

V–VI; occasionally V–IV. In this cadence V resolves to a substitute for I in circumstances in which I is strongly expected. The cadence provides an accent (harmonically) with the arrival of VI, and it often has the effect of a musical surprise. It is a common means of facilitating the extension of the phrase by delaying the appearance of the V–I cadence normally expected.

Example 4

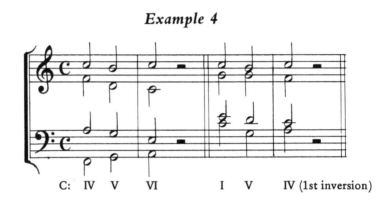

C: IV V VI   I V   IV (1st inversion)

Plagal

IV–I. The plagal cadence is occasionally called the "amen" cadence. There is a finality about the plagal cadence, but it is not by any means as commonly used as the authentic cadence. It is often used as an extension of the phrase because it frequently occurs immediately after an authentic cadence progression.

Example 5

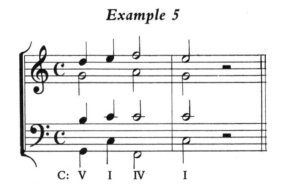

C: V I IV   I

One additional type of cadence occurs with some frequency in music of the Baroque era. It is called the *Phrygian cadence*, and it is usually used to conclude a slow movement or shorter portion of music. It occurs only in the minor mode and involves the progression IV (in first inversion) to V. Although this cadence ends on V, there is considerable finality about it. However, it is not likely to be used as the final cadence in a piece, because such cadences are usually followed by a faster movement in the same key.

Example 6

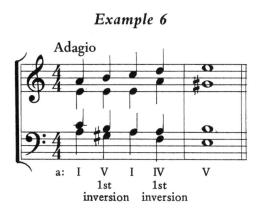

PHRASE ENDINGS

The conclusion of the phrase also involves an accentual pattern that is referred to as the *phrase ending*. There are two kinds:

Masculine, in which the final chord of the phrase (and consequently the last chord of the cadence formula) occurs on the accented beat of the measure;
Feminine, in which the final chord of the phrase (and consequently the last chord of the cadence formula) occurs on the unaccented portion of the measure.

Example 7

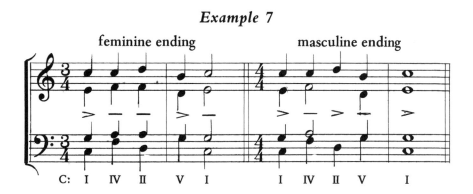

There is no correlation between the type of cadence and the choice of phrase ending. Both are largely the result of melodic considerations.

ANALYZING THE PHRASE STRUCTURE OF A PIECE

In order to analyze any piece it is necessary to play it over many times to gain familiarity with it. This is an easy task with the piece that is shown in Example 8, a setting of "America" that dates from 1740.

Note: The Roman numeral analysis of Example 8 indicates, as you are accustomed to doing, the root of each chord. Some of the chords are inverted and are so marked (see Chapter 4). Some of the V chords contain an additional B flat. The analytical symbols to explain these features have not been included in this analysis because we have not yet discussed them. The symbol [ˌ] has been used to mark the ends of the phrases.

Example 8

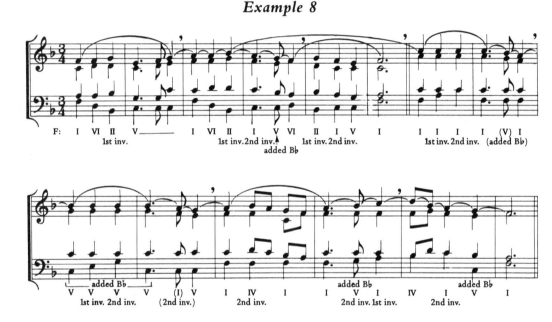

We note that the melody divides into seven phrases, each two measures long. On closer examination, we also note that:

The first three phrases are concerned with a stepwise ascent from the initial F in the soprano melody (the highest note is B flat), followed by a stepwise return to the F. Also, F persists in the third phrase.

The fourth phrase begins on the highest note thus far, and this note has been prepared by (bears a stepwise relation to) the B flat in measure three.

There is a stepwise descent from that C to G at the end of the fifth phrase.

The sixth phrase rises from A to C again, and the final phrase descends with a flourish (the D–B flat chord tone leap of a third) rapidly to the final F.

From the standpoint of melodic repetition, the second phrase bears a close resemblance to the first phrase (it is stated up a third, but the direction of the last three notes is reversed). The third phrase is simply an approach to an important inner cadence that divides the piece. The fourth and fifth phrases are identical to each other, with the fifth phrase simply a transposition of the fourth phrase, down a step. The four repeated notes in these two phrases provide a contrast with what has gone on before. The general downward direction of the line in the fourth and fifth phrases contrasts with the rising and falling shape of the first three phrases, and with the rising and falling shape of the sixth and seventh phrases. A melodic profile might be shown as follows:

Example 9

The first cadence of Example 8 is a half cadence (the phrase moves essentially from I–V). The second phrase ends with a deceptive cadence that thrusts the music forward energetically (in a way that could not have been done by an authentic cadence here). The third cadence is one of great finality, a perfect authentic cadence (the second-most final cadence of the piece). Following this, the harmonic rhythm slows dramatically, essentially retaining the tonic chord for two measures (passing tones in the soprano and alto do momentarily suggest V), and a single dominant chord (with passing tonic inflection) is used in the next two measures. Thus the fourth and fifth melodic phrases have been harmonically bound together as a single tonic to dominant progression, forming a grand half cadence. The harmonic rhythm of the first section returns in the last two phrases, the first of which ends in an imperfect authentic cadence, with the final cadence (as we would expect), a perfect authentic cadence.

Each of the phrases of Example 8 begins with a primary triad (I, IV, or V), except for the third phrase, which begin with II in first inversion. The triad II, built on a tonal degree, exerts considerable tonal strength in this progression. Harmonic color is added by the occasional use of VI and II in midphrase in the first section, and the triad III does not appear at all. It is also interesting to note that IV does not make an appearance until the last two phrases.

Summary of the Phrase Structure

1. Each phrase is begun with tonal strength.
2. Both the repetition structure of the melody and the contrasts within it are underscored by the harmonic choices.

a. The first measure and the third measure are identical in chords and inversions.

b. The deceptive cadence keeps the music from coming to a premature authentic cadence at a point where the melody wants to go on to an important cadence.

c. The contrasting melodic section, with its repeated notes and descending line, is underscored by a drastic slowing of harmonic rhythm. The static harmony is further underscored by the C that persists in the tenor (pedal tone) for more than four measures.

d. A strong new element (IV) is introduced to make the approach to the final cadence as emphatic as possible.

PERTAINING TO PART III EXAMPLES

All of the musical examples in Part III consist of phrases that can serve to illustrate the information of this chapter. Particularly clear examples of authentic cadences (both perfect and imperfect), half, and deceptive cadences are provided in Example One. The cadences in this example and in Example Two are conveniently identified by the use of fermata signs, a practice common in early chorale editions. Examine the two pieces phrase by phrase, noting particularly where triads other than I, IV, and V occur.

EXERCISES

1. With a chord to precede, in the keys indicated below, construct in four parts the following kinds of cadences: perfect authentic, imperfect authentic, half, deceptive, and plagal.

E flat major	g minor
D major	b minor
A major	f sharp minor
B flat major	c minor

2. Analyze each of the following bass lines to determine the kind of cadence called for at each phrase ending, and label each. After doing this, make a four-part root-progression harmonization of each bass line.

3. Make a Roman numeral analysis of Example One (if you have not done so already) and of Example Two from Part III. Identify all of the cadences in each.

4. Make a Roman numeral analysis of every chord you can identify in Example Five from Part III. Mark the phrases and identify all cadences. (*Note:* The left-hand accompaniment will simplify the task of Roman numeral analysis.)

5. In Example Seven from Part III, mark all of the phrases and identify all cadences.

CHAPTER 10

First Inversion and Figured Bass

FIRST INVERSION

Any triad arranged so that its third is placed as its lowest note is said to be in first inversion. The other two members of the triad are intervals of a third and a sixth (or a compound of these intervals) above the lowest note. It does not matter which of the other two members of the triad is above the other; all that matters in first inversion is that the third of the triad is the lowest note.

The first-inversion triad expands the available harmonic resources in at least two quite practical ways: (1) it is useful in providing a lighter feeling instead of the somewhat heavier sound of a succession of root-progression harmonies; (2) it also makes it easier to write a bass line that can move by step, thereby making possible a better melodic line in the bass.

It is important to realize that the first inversion is not the equivalent of a root position, even though it is often possible to use it where otherwise a root position might be used. The first-inversion triad cannot be used in a perfect authentic cadence and therefore is not usually found as one of the last two chords of a piece. In fact, because cadences are points of harmonic strength, first inversions are generally not as suitable as root positions for the final chords of phrases.

Since one of its functions is to create stepwise motion in the bass line, the bass note of a first-inversion triad should have a stepwise relationship to at least one of the other bass notes around it. Therefore, one is less likely to use a first inversion if its bass note is approached by leap and left by leap. In that sense, first inversions differ from root-position triads. An exception to this occurs when the bass leaps from the root position to the first inversion of the same triad, and this is a circumstance that is quite common.

Example 1

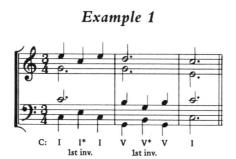

The following example (Example 2) compares the relatively heavy sound of root progression with the same progression using a reasonable number of first inversions. The root-progression bass (on the left), because of continual leaps, takes on a heaviness, even an awkwardness, that might not be desired. The example (on the right) that introduces a few first inversions has more of a sense of motion toward the cadence for two reasons: (1) the root of V in the cadence has been approached by a stepwise line; and (2) the strength of the perfect authentic cadence stands out more clearly because it has been preceded by the less stable sound of the first inversions.

Example 2

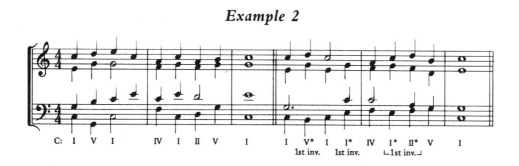

The use of any triad, whether it is in root position or inverted, is best determined by experiment and practice. The following generalizations are offered as an initial guide. The common designation for root position, as we know, is the use of the Roman numeral indicating the scale degree of the triad root. The common designation for first inversion is the appropriate Roman numeral (identifying the root) and the number 6. The use of numbers to indicate triad position will be explained later in this chapter.

I$_6$ provides the sound of tonic harmony in a less stable form than the root position; it avoids a strong cadential feeling where desired (that is, in midphrase).

II$_6$ is often used to lead into a cadence because it proceeds in the bass by step to V (II$_6$–V–I); as such it is just as commonly found in cadence formulas as IV.

III$_6$ is a weaker triad than V, but sounds quite a bit like it because it contains two notes of the V chord and the dominant of the scale is the lowest note of III$_6$.

IV$_6$ provides the sound of subdominant harmony in a less stable form than root position; moreover, it permits the bass to move down by step to the root of a dominant triad in a cadence formula (IV$_6$–V–I).

V$_6$ is useful where the finality of a perfect authentic cadence is not desired or where it is desirable to avoid a cadence altogether (as in midphrase). It provides stepwise movement to the tonic (in the bass) since the leading tone must be resolved.

VI$_6$ is a weaker triad than I, but sounds quite a bit like it because it contains two notes of the tonic triad and the tonic of the scale is the lowest note of VI$_6$.

VII$_6$ functions like a dominant; it can substitute for V where V is less viable from a standpoint of voice leading. It is a frequent passing chord from I to I$_6$, or the reverse.

DOUBLING AND FIRST INVERSIONS

The rules for doubling are not particularly changed by the introduction of first inversions, except that in a first inversion the root will usually not be doubled unless it is a tonal degree.

Revised Rules for Doubling

Root position: Double the root, or double a tonal degree.
First inversion: Double a tonal degree (1,2,4,5), unless good voice leading shows another doubling to be better.

No new voice-leading rules are necessary in using first-inversion triads. It is still desirable to avoid ambiguity by moving each voice to the nearest note of the next chord and by holding over common tones wherever possible. Remember also to resolve leading tones, unless very good melodic justification permits another treatment.

Example 3

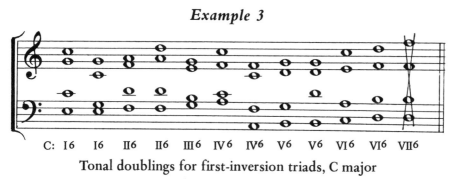

C: I6   I6   II6   II6   III6   IV6   IV6   V6   V6   VI6   VI6   VII6

Tonal doublings for first-inversion triads, C major

A word of caution is appropriate for the triad VII$_6$. Even though the fourth degree of the scale (F in the example above) is a tonal degree, it is a poor choice for doubling unless there is a good melodic reason for that doubling. The fourth degree forms a dissonance (augmented fourth or diminished fifth) with the root of the triad (B in the example above). In general, it is not desirable to double a note that forms a dissonance with another note of the same triad.

THE FIGURED BASS

The figured bass (also called thorough bass) was a shorthand method of indicating harmonies (and even voice leading) for a keyboard accompaniment. It was generally used during the Baroque period, and players of keyboard instruments were able to perform from the figured bass score, realizing at sight relatively elaborate and complex musical settings. The skilled performer was able to improvise musical ideas that were based on themes and motives of other voices or instruments within the ensemble. While figured bass writing is not used by composers today, it is a common and convenient means of indicating harmony. It is also an important method by which one can become familiar with a process that is essential to an understanding of music by Bach and Handel, as well as the music of other Baroque composers.

In the Baroque era, the figured bass contained only the notated bass lines along with any Arabic numbers (no Roman numerals) representing inversions. The Roman numerals were unnecessary since the bass line was already present, and the absence of any numbers was an indication of root position. The figures we will use—both Roman numerals and Arabic numbers—are thus adapted from historical practice.

CHORD SYMBOLS FOR TRIADS

The numbers that are placed beside the Roman numeral designating a triad are used as shown in Example 4 to indicate root position, first inversion, and second inversion:

Example 4

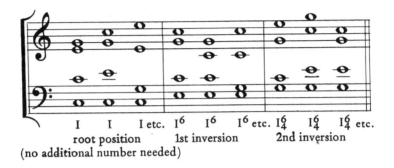

Full numbering of a root-position triad is $\frac{5}{3}$, numbering that indicates notes a third and a fifth above the given bass. It is common practice in using figured basses not to use any figures at all for root positions since a Roman numeral without numbers can be assumed to indicate a root-position triad.

Full numbering for a first-inversion triad is $\frac{6}{3}$, which indicates notes a third and a sixth above the given bass. In common practice, the first inversion is usually indicated by a 6 alone. Similarly, the designation $\frac{6}{4}$ indicates a second-inversion triad. In common practice, both the 6 and the 4 are used for the indication of second inversions.

Summary of Chord Symbols for Triads

Triad Position	*Full Numbering*	*Common Practice*
root position	$\frac{5}{3}$	no numbers
first inversion	$\frac{6}{3}$	6
second inversion	$\frac{6}{4}$	$\frac{6}{4}$

Other numbers can be used in figured bass designations, and these simply refer to a specific interval above the bass where either a fourth chord tone (or a nonchord tone) should be placed. A chromatic alteration *by itself* (without a numeral) assumes the interval of a third above the bass note, just as would be the case if the numeral 3 had been indicated. That means that an accidental is indicated for the note that is a third above the bass.

Example 5

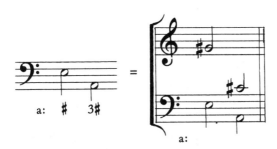

A chromatic alteration beside a number refers to the alteration of that note placed above the bass at the interval indicated by the figure. In the Baroque era, a slash through a number had the same effect as placing a sharp beside that number, thus raising the note indicated by a half step.

Example 6 shows a simple figured bass, followed by its four-part realization in a musical score. You will notice the use of the number 6 with a slash through it; this is exactly the same as indicating 6♯. Further, you will notice the numbers 8 and 7, which refer, as do all of the other numbers, to the placement of notes by specific intervals above the given bass.

Example 6

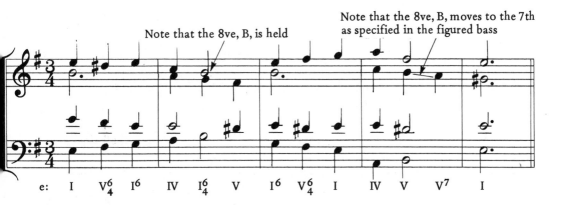

PERTAINING TO PART III EXAMPLES

Examine the use of first-inversion triads in Examples Two, Five, and Seven.

1. Count the number of first inversions and compare their frequency with the number of root-position triads.
2. Count the number of second inversions. What conclusions can you come to regarding frequency of second inversions?
3. Write out the root-position bass line that would have existed if no inversions had been used.
4. Notice where the inverted triads are placed within each phrase.

EXERCISES

1.   a.   Derive a figured bass from the following hymn by Vincent Novello.
         1) Copy the bass line on a sheet of manuscript paper; do not add Roman numerals.
         2) Place under each note the numerical symbol appropriate to indicate the inversion of the chord at hand or, if it is in root position, put no symbol.

Vincent Novello, 1800

"Albano" by Vincent Novello. Reprinted from *The Hymnal of the Protestant Episcopal Church, 1940,* prepared by the Joint Commission on the Hymnal. Copyright 1940 by the Church Pension Fund, N.Y.

          3) You know that the numbers you are using indicate notes a specific interval above the given bass. If there are more than three different notes in a particular chord or if there is a note that does not seem to be part of the triad, simply count the interval by which that note is above the bass and write the number under the bass note over which the additional note occurs.
     b.   Derive a figured bass for Example Two, Part III, following the instructions just given for exercise 1a.
2.   Realize the following figured bass lines in four parts. The numbers are in the correct format for figured bass; however, before you begin, place the appropriate Roman numeral beneath each bass note. If no Arabic numbers are used, the chord is in root position.

3. Harmonize the following bass lines, using root-position triads and triads in first inversion as appropriate. Label each line with the appropriate Roman numerals and Arabic numbers.

CHAPTER 11

Dominant and Nondominant Sevenths

Up to this point, the study of chords has been concerned with triads—chords of three tones, built in superposed thirds. But chords are not limited to three tones, and composers have consistently made other chordal structures by placing additional tones (in the form of superposed thirds) on top of the basic three-note triad.

Most common among these other chordal structures is the *seventh chord*. It is formed by placing an additional tone a third above the fifth of the triad. This additional tone forms the interval of a seventh with the bass, and it is for this reason that such chords are called seventh chords. In short, a seventh can be added to any triad, and seventh chords can be built on any scale degree.

CHORD SYMBOLS FOR SEVENTH CHORDS

The system for adding numbers to Roman numerals for the designation of triads and their inversions explained in the previous chapter can now be expanded to include the numbers that are used to indicate seventh chords and their inversions.

7th Chord Position	*Full Numbering*	*Common Practice*
	7	
root position	5	7
	3	

first inversion	6 5 3	6 5
second inversion	6 4 3	4 3
third inversion	6 4 2	$\frac{4}{2}$ or 2

Notice in this chart that the numbers indicate an additional tone; this is necessary because there are four tones in a seventh chord instead of the three one finds in a triad. As a result, an additional inversion becomes possible.

While the basic principles of voice leading remain unchanged, certain characteristics of the various kinds of seventh chords will be discussed below. Common to all seventh chords, however, is the fact that the seventh of the chord forms a tension, or a dissonance, with the root of the chord. The normal resolution of that dissonance is for the seventh to move down by half step (or whole step). Moreover, since four different chord tones are possible within the chord, it is not essential to double a tone of the chord as we have done in triads. Nonetheless, in root position it is not unusual to double the root of seventh chords, in which case the fifth of the chord is normally omitted.

Example 1

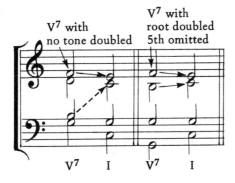

Caution: Do not become confused by terminology that refers to the "seventh" of a chord and the "seventh" degree of a scale: (1) The seventh of a chord is the note found the interval of a seventh above the chord root, when the chord is in root position. That seventh normally resolves down by half step or whole step. (2) The seventh degree of a scale is the leading tone of the scale (it is also the third of a V chord), and its normal resolution is up by half step.

THE DOMINANT SEVENTH CHORD

Seventh chords present a new variety of sonorities and functions. The most important of all seventh chords is the Dominant seventh. This chord (V_7) is a dominant triad to which has been added the tone a minor seventh above the root. (A minor seventh above the root of the dominant triad is the fourth degree of the scale, and this is the tone that results from superposing an additional third to the dominant triad.) More simply, V_7 is a major triad to which has been added the tone a minor seventh above the root. In its complete form no tone needs to be doubled (in four-part writing) since there are four separate tones in the chord: root, third (leading tone), fifth, and seventh. This is a complex chord that has a powerful tendency to resolve to the tonic triad.

Tendencies

We have encountered both melodic and harmonic tendencies in the study of harmony up to this point. We have observed the drive inherent in a leading tone to move to its tonic. This, then, is a tendency tone: a tone which seeks to resolve to a more stable tone. We have also observed, in the chapter on cadences, the inevitable expectation for a dominant triad to move to its tonic triad. As we have stated before, the dominant to tonic movement is the strongest progression in harmony.

Melodic movement by half step can, of itself, generate a feeling of tendency. For example, the leading tone and the fourth degree of the scale are a dissonant interval apart, an augmented fourth (called a *tritone* because it consists of three whole steps), or its inversion, the diminished fifth. These dissonant intervals generate a tendency to resolve to a more consonant interval. As Example 2 shows, the tendency of an augmented fourth is to expand to a sixth, and the tendency of a diminished fifth is to contract to a third.

Example 2

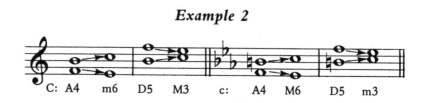

By adding the minor seventh above the root of a dominant triad, the diminished fifth (tritone) dissonance becomes a part of the chord; furthermore, the seventh of the dominant seventh chord is the fourth degree of the scale (which, in this context, tends to resolve to the third degree of the scale). The result is that much of the voice leading by which V_7 moves to the next chord is predetermined.

Resolution of the Dominant Seventh Chord

The resolution is V_7–I, just as V–I has been used previously to resolve the dominant chord. The leading tone resolves up; the seventh resolves down (to the third degree of the tonic triad); and the common tones, if any, are held over. *Note:* In the root progression V_7–I, it is often not practical to resolve a complete V_7 to a complete I (particularly if the leading tone of V is in the soprano or if there is wide spacing in the progression). Instead, the following two possibilities present themselves:

1. In root position: V_7, with all four tones present, resolves to I with the fifth omitted (three roots and a third).

Example 3

C: V^7 I
complete

2. (The reverse of the above is the second possibility.) In root position: V_7, with root doubled and fifth omitted, will resolve to I with all three of its tones present.

Example 4

C: V^7 I
complete

Of course, another possibility exists if the leading tone is not in the soprano: that is for the voice above to take over the leading-tone note of resolution, so that the leading tone may leap down by a third to the fifth of the tonic triad, as was explained in Chapter 8.

Example 5

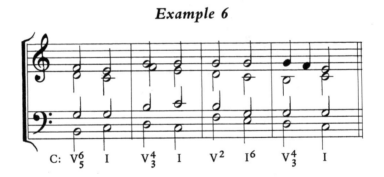

Inversions of V_7 offer somewhat more flexibility since both the dominant seventh chord and the tonic chord can be complete. The resolutions and chord symbols for inversions of V_7 are shown in Example 6.

Example 6

Note that in each of these resolutions the leading tone of V_7 resolves upwards by step (or resolves as in Example 5), and the seventh of the chord resolves down. The V_7 chord may also resolve to VI (as in a deceptive cadence) because the tendency tones can be resolved correctly.

Example 7

Passing-Tone Seventh

The seventh may also be introduced as a tone that passes between the fifth and the third degrees of the scale in the progression V–I. This causes the seventh to appear as a moving part between the two chords.

Example 8

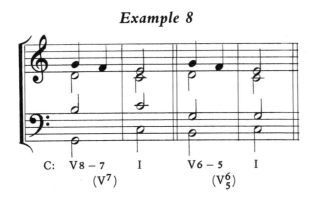

C: V8 – 7   I   V6 – 5   I
        (V⁷)   (V⁶₅)

Note the use of the figures 8–7 and 6–5 in Example 8. Melodic movement in a single voice was often specified in such a way in the historical use of the figured bass, and it is an indication with which harmony students should be familiar. The 8–7 indicates that in an upper voice (not necessarily the top voice) there is movement from a note an octave above the bass note to a note a seventh above the bass (in this case, G to F). In the second part of the example, the numbers 6–5 accomplish the same melodic movement (the numbers are different because the bass note in the inversion is not the same as it was in root position).

NONDOMINANT SEVENTH CHORDS

Just as a seventh may be added above the root of a dominant triad, a seventh may also be added above the roots of other triads in the scale. Such chords vary in structure and sound, depending on the particular scale degree that serves as the root of the chord. In spite of their diversity, some theorists have called all these chords nondominant seventh chords, treating them as a class in order to differentiate them from the V_7 chord to which they bear some resemblance.

Some of the differences are noted below:

1. Dominant sevenths have a leading tone that is the third of the chord (and of course, a seventh chord built on VII would be dominant in function,[1] with the leading tone as root); there is no leading tone functioning in a nondominant seventh.

1. See Chapter 16.

2. Dominant sevenths have a tone a minor seventh above the root; the seventh above the root in nondominant sevenths is sometimes a major seventh and sometimes a minor seventh, depending on the scale degree on which the root has been placed.

3. Dominant sevenths contain the interval of a tritone (as does also the seventh chord built on VII, which is dominant in function),[2] and both of the pitches forming the tritone require resolution; nondominant sevenths do not contain that tritone function, with the exception of II in minor keys.

4. Dominant triads (in major and minor keys using the harmonic form of the minor scale) are always major triads; nondominant sevenths are built on triads that may be any of the four forms (MmAd).

5. Dominant sevenths are a combination of a major triad and a minor seventh; nondominant sevenths do not produce this combination.[3]

In short, when one encounters the combination of a major triad and a minor seventh in tonal music, that chord will almost invariably be dominant in function. Using the unaltered major scale, or using the unaltered harmonic form of the minor scale, it is only possible to construct a dominant seventh chord on the fifth degree of the scale.[4] Thus, the dominant seventh is unique within its key.

Note: Seventh chords built on the leading tone of the scale are quite likely to have a dominant function (diminished seventh and half-diminished chords), which will be explained in Chapter 16.

Example 9 shows nondominant sevenths built on every scale degree in major and minor keys. One can observe the considerable diversity of structure that is characteristic of nondominant sevenths.

Example 9

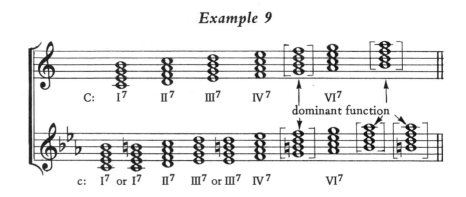

2. See Chapter 16.

3. However, if the natural minor scale is used, a major triad and a minor seventh can be built on the seventh degree of the scale (B♭ DFA ♭ in c minor); similarly, using the ascending form of the melodic minor scale, such a combination can be built on the fourth degree of the scale (FACE♭ in c minor). Both of these would function as secondary dominants (see Chapter 15).

4. See Chapter 15.

The regular resolution of nondominant sevenths chords is by root movement up a fourth or down a fifth, and the most common irregular resolution is by root movement up a second. Always remember that the seventh is a tendency tone in nondominant sevenths as well as in dominant sevenths—as a dissonant tone, it usually resolves down a second.

Example 10

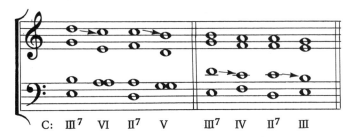

The interval of a *major* seventh (as opposed to a minor seventh) is quite dissonant and should be used with restraint. The seventh in such cases often produces a better effect if it is used as a passing tone.

Example 11

When a chain of seventh chords appears in root position, one must be careful to avoid parallel fifths. One technique for doing this is to double the root of every other chord, omitting the fifth.

Example 12

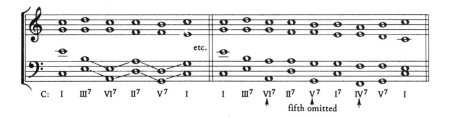

PERTAINING TO PART III EXAMPLES

Example Three contains many dominant seventh chords and non-dominant seventh chords. Each chord is clearly arpeggiated (that is, one note is played at a time), and there is only one chord change per measure. Non-dominant sevenths may be found in measures 2, 8, 9, 16, 17 and 21. The V_7 chord is found in measures 3, 18, 24, 27, 31, and (over a pedal-tone C in the bass) 34. There are a number of chords present in Example Three that have not yet been explained; for this reason, the analysis should be restricted to the measures indicated and may include any other portions which are easily understood.

EXERCISES

1. a. With a chord of your choice to precede the resolution, resolve V_7 to I in the following keys (in four parts):

    A flat major
    B major
    f sharp minor
    b flat minor
    c sharp minor
    E flat major

    b. Repeat the assignment above, this time resolving V_5^6 to I.

2. Harmonize the following progressions in four parts. You must also determine where you would like to have the phrases end (placing the cadences); and you must determine the duration of each chord, as well as deciding where the barlines should be placed.

    Ab: $\frac{3}{4}$ I I$_6$ II$_6$ V$_7$ VI IV II V$_7$ I I$_6$ III IV V$_7$ VI VI$_6$ I IV$_6$ V$_7$ I

3. Realize the following figured basses in four parts. The figured bass numbers are correct in format; however, before you begin, place the appropriate Roman numeral beneath each bass note.

4. Construct, in four-part harmony, the following sequence of root-position seventh chords:

$$\text{I III}_7\text{ VI}_7\text{ II}_7\text{ V}_7\text{ I}_7\text{ IV}_7\text{ V}_7\text{ I}$$

Do this first in the key of D major, and then do it a second time in the key of B flat major.

CHAPTER 12

Harmonization
of Melodies

One of the most difficult and important aspects of harmony is learning how to harmonize a melody. Only those who can improvise intuitively can avoid the process of trial and error. However, it is possible to minimize the problems of harmonizing by a systematic approach that, as a first step, seeks to identify the most apparent harmonic implications in melodies. The subject of how to harmonize cannot be treated comprehensively at this time, but we can make a beginning. Further aspects of the process will be presented at appropriate points in the text.

FIRST STEP

Play the melody over several times until you are fully acquainted with it. Identify the key; become familiar with its phrase divisions; and locate and identify all of its cadences.

SECOND STEP

Sketch in the Roman numerals for the progressions that occur at the cadences. There should be little difficulty in doing this because cadence formulas are limited. The last note of each phrase (and the note preceding it) will ordinarily indicate whether the cadence is to be a half cadence or an authentic cadence. If there is doubt, try both types and select the one you decide is the more appropriate. Of course, there is no doubt about wanting a perfect authentic cadence for the end of the melody.

THIRD STEP

Leaps within a measure proceeding from a beat that is accented to a beat that is unaccented often imply or outline a chord containing both of the notes involved. If the melody is in triple meter, in which only the first beat is accented, any leap *within* a measure (not across the barline) is likely to outline a single chord. As a first choice, sketch in the Roman numerals that are suggested by all such leaps from strong to weak beats, or from one weak beat to another. Crossing a barline generally requires a change of chord because such movement is from an unaccented beat to one that is accented. The only exception to this is in the case of a pickup to a phrase (anacrusis), in which case the harmony is frequently retained across the first barline of the phrase, as a kind of harmonic anticipation.

Example 1

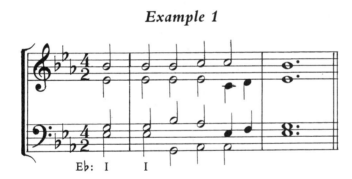

FOURTH STEP

Decide on the probable frequency of chord change. With the exception of the anacrusis, the chord will almost always change across a barline, even if a repeated melodic note is involved. The chords usually change on a rather regular basis, often on every beat or on every metric accent. Because there are three different notes in every triad, it is theoretically possible to choose three different chords to harmonize any given melodic note. However, as a first step, it will simplify matters to choose one of the primary triads—I, IV, or V—for each melodic note (since every degree of the scale can be accommodated by at least one of the primary triads). If this choice should feel inadequate, one should try experimenting with the other triads that are possibilities for each of the melodic notes (choosing from II, III, VI, or VII). It will be helpful, in

choosing a substitute for one of the primary triads, to remember the summary
of strong progressions presented in Chapter 7 and to remember that the
supertonic triad (II) is a frequently used chord. With this in mind, sketch in a
simple root-progression bass line. Don't forget to change from a root position
to a first inversion when variety is needed, but a change of chord seems
unnecessary.

FIFTH STEP

Try to build a more stepwise bass line by introducing first inversions. If a
lighter texture appears to be needed at any point, experiment with the
possibility of using a first inversion. Constantly compare the bass with the
soprano in order to make sure that there are no voice-leading problems such as
parallel octaves or fifths. Always check to make sure that you resolve any
leading tones that may occur in the bass. Complete the harmonization by
filling in the inner voices. Be careful not to double an inappropriate note.

Example 2

Now try the sample harmonization problem in Example 2, demonstrating each
of the steps outlined above.

Step One

In the melody shown in Example 2, it is apparent that the key is G major.
(The key signature is one sharp, and the two most important cadences—at
measures 5 and 10—end on the note G.)

Step Two

There are four cadences that can be identified (see Example 3). The first
cadence (at the end of measure 2) is a half cadence, and the chords for this
cadence will therefore be I–V. The second cadence (measures 4 and 5) is an
authentic cadence, and the chords for this cadence will be V–I. The third
cadence (measure 7) is another half cadence. Note that the F sharp–D leap,
from strong beat to weak, outlines the dominant chord, which means that the
dominant chord arrives on the third beat of that measure. (The A that occurs
on the second beat of measure 7 will *not* be harmonized with V, but with a

chord that leads well into V, like II.) The final cadence at the end of the piece is melodically the same as the second cadence, and it will logically also be an authentic cadence. Because it is the last cadence of the piece, it will be a perfect authentic cadence.

Example 3

Step Three

By examining the melody for all leaps that proceed from an *accented* beat to an *unaccented* beat (see Example 4), we find several outlined harmonies. *Measure 1:* The leap from beat 1 to beat 2 outlines the harmony of I, and the leap from beat 3 to beat 4 outlines the harmony of V. *Measure 2:* The leap from beat 1 to beat 2 outlines I again (or possibly VI, if one should decide not to repeat I so soon). *Measure 3:* Beats 3 and 4 seem to imply the harmony of IV. *Measure 7:* The leap from beat 3 to beat 4 has already (in the decision about cadences) been shown to outline V. *Measure 8:* Beats 3 and 4 are identical to measure 3, and the harmony of IV seems to be implied. The only other leap in the melody occurs in measure 7, from beat 2 to beat 3 (from weak to strong beat, which does not outline a chord).

Example 4

Step Four

The remaining melodic notes, for which we have not yet chosen chords, have the possibility of being harmonized by three different chords for each note (see Example 5). With a melody like this, moving in quarter notes at a moderate tempo, it is likely that the chords should change on almost every quarter note. This is not to say that the chord must change on every beat, for we have already retained a single chord for two beats where leaps have apparently outlined chords, but we should at least explore the possibility of changing the chord on every beat for the notes remaining.

Example 5

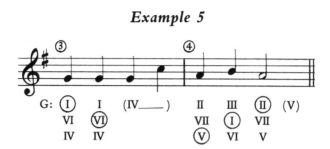

The encircled Roman numerals in Example 5 present a possible solution, but by no means the only possible solution. These chords have been chosen by following the guidelines suggested in the summary of strong progressions (Chapter 7) and by using primary triads as much as possible. Other triads have been introduced only to add color or to avoid an undesired repetition of harmonies. The VII chord has been avoided as a choice because V is preferred to VII unless it would make better voice leading to use VII instead of V. Note that when melodic notes are repeated, the harmony has been changed in order to avoid a static area in the musical movement.

Note these specific chord choices. *Measure 4:* On the third beat the harmony of II is used to approach the V–I cadence, so that V will not occur on two successive beats while the half note is held in the melody. *Measures 3 and 8:* As we will see in step 5 (Example 7), II has been chosen as a substitute for IV on the fourth beat of these measures partly for the additional harmonic color it provides and partly because of looking ahead to the making of a better bass line. Since measures 3 and 4 have the same melody as measures 8 and 9, a simple solution is to use the same harmonization for both. At this stage the following root position bass emerges

Example 6

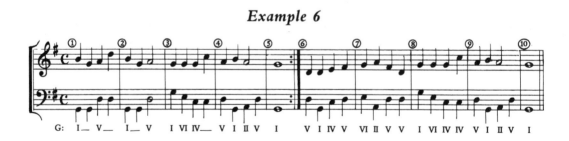

Step Five

First inversions have been used in measures 1 and 2 (see Example 7) to provide a sense of movement where no change of chord is needed, and the same is true in the first two beats of measure 8. To provide contrary motion between bass and soprano, VI was chosen instead of IV on beat 3 of measure 6, and IV was chosen instead of VI on beat 1 of measure 7. Other first inversions have been introduced to create a better bass melody. As mentioned earlier, at the end of measure 3 and at the end of measure 8, II has replaced IV in order to provide a better approach to V_6. The use of V_6 avoids a feeling of premature finality that might have been experienced with a root-position dominant chord at this point.

Example 7

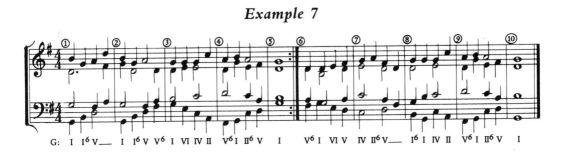

The most musical solution of this harmonization problem should involve the use of nonharmonic tones to fill in leaps and to decorate repeated notes. We will return to this problem in the next chapter (which deals with nonharmonic tones) in order to demonstrate a more complete and a more musical harmonization.

EXERCISES

Make a four-part harmonization of each of the following soprano lines. In each case, write out separately each of the five steps outlined in this chapter. Use V_7 where appropriate.

CHAPTER 13

Nonharmonic Tones and the Six-Four Chord

In the previous chapter, using simple melodic lines, we began to seek ways by which we could identify some of the harmonic implications that are present in all tonal melodies. The melodies in Chapter 12 are chorale-like; that is to say, they are simple in structure and generally require a change of chord on every note or two. In such melodies the notes possess a relatively equal importance in relation to one another. Harmonically one could say that the notes of such melodies are nearly all of the same structural significance, and thus each note deserves to be harmonized.

In most music, however, one finds melodies that also contain less important notes, and these customarily (with good musical effect) may escape being harmonized. Example 1 contrasts two melodic phrases that illustrate, on the one hand, a basic melodic line (which is a chorale melody), and, on the other, an elaboration of that same melody by the addition of a great many less important notes. The first melody has been harmonized by Bach in a hymn-like choral version; the second is a more elaborate version of the same melody, written by Bach for the organ, in which the decorative notes do not effectively alter the harmonic implications of the basic melodic line.

Example 1

Bach, Wenn wir in höchsten Nöthen sein

Melodic notes, within a more elaborate melody, gain importance by a variety of means:

1. By emphasizing a single note by placing it on an accented beat;
2. By obviously repeating a note;
3. By placing a note as the goal of a stepwise or chromatic lineal movement;
4. By outlining a specific chord with notes that leap from strong (accented) to weak (unaccented), or from weak to weak within a measure (as in Example 2);
5. By placing a note at the turning point of a melodic line.

Example 2

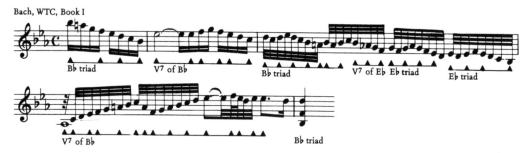

Bach, WTC, Book I

The material of this chapter will deal with the common categories of notes that do not receive direct harmonic support and will explain their function in relation to the chords against which they are sounding.

CONSONANCE AND DISSONANCE

A note that is part of a major or minor triad is consonant with the other notes of that triad. Conversely, a note that is sounding with that triad, but is not a part of it, is a dissonant note. The consonant intervals are P8, P5, P4, P unison, M6, m6, M3, and m3. All of these intervals can be found within the structure of a major triad, as shown in Example 3.

Example 3

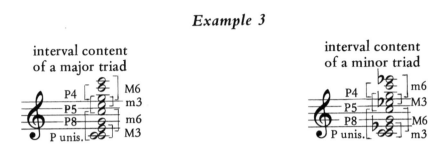

interval content
of a major triad

interval content
of a minor triad

We have already encountered two intervals that are dissonant, even though they belong to chords used with great frequency. They are the tritone intervals—the augmented fourth and its inversion, the diminished fifth. These intervals, found in VII and V_7, possess an inherent tension that causes them to seek stepwise resolution to the following consonant intervals.

Example 4

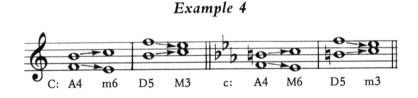

The terms *consonance* and *dissonance* have come to be used descriptively to indicate a quality of sound. Consonance refers to sounds that present a sense of stability (the degree of stability varies depending on whether the consonances are perfect or imperfect). Dissonance refers to sounds that present some sense of instability and on many occasions may be associated with a strident sound quality.

NONHARMONIC TONES

The term *nonharmonic tone* literally means a note that is not a part of the chord against which it is sounding. Instead of implying a quality of sound, like harshness, the term refers to a category of dissonant (unstable) melodic notes that function in different ways. These nonharmonic tones are of the following types: passing tones, neighbor notes (auxiliaries), appoggiaturas, suspensions, pedal tones, échappées, cambiatas, and anticipations.

We know that melodies may imply harmonies by outlining chords. The role of the leap was discussed in this regard. However, it is also true that stepwise passages may represent leaps which have been filled in. The harmonic implications of such filled-in leaps are basically the same as those of the leaps themselves, because passing tones are used to connect the triad pitches. In Example 5 the first two measures involve an arpeggiation of the tonic triad, while the third measure leaps from one note to another of the V chord. Note that the passing tones occur on unaccented portions of the measure.

Example 5

C: I   V   I

Passing Tone

The passing tone is an unaccented nonchordal tone that fills in a leap of a third (see Example 6). Double passing tones may fill in the leap of a fourth on an unaccented beat.[1] The function of the passing tone is to carry the melodic line by step from one chord tone to another. Passing tones may be indicated by using a plus sign (+).

Example 6

C: V   +   I   + +

Neighbor Note or Auxiliary

The neighbor note is an unaccented nonchordal tone that is approached by step from above or below and that returns by step to the original tone (see Example 7). The function of the neighbor note is to elaborate what is essentially a repeated or a sustained tone. Neighbor notes may be indicated by using the sign ✕.

---

1.   Tones that fill in leaps, in the manner of passing tones, but occur on an accented beat, or on the accented portion of an unaccented beat, are often called *accented passing tones*. Their function is that of a "prepared" appoggiatura and will be discussed under that category of nonharmonic tone.

Example 7

It is also possible to use both the upper and lower neighbor notes together as a single ornamentation, called the double neighbor (or double auxiliary).

Example 8

Appoggiatura

The appoggiatura is an *accented* nonchordal tone that resolves—usually down—by step (see Example 9). The note of resolution must be unaccented in relation to the appoggiatura itself. It is also possible for the appoggiatura to resolve upward, in which case the resolution is usually by half step. The function of the appoggiatura is to displace the note to which it resolves, in effect inflecting that note by delaying its appearance. The appoggiatura occurs on an accented portion of the measure and may function as an accented passing tone,[2] or it may be preceded by a leap. It is generally not good practice to sound the pitch of resolution (in another voice) at the same time as the appoggiatura is sounding, unless that resolution pitch is in the bass. This is because such a doubling tends to lessen the full effect of delaying the appearance of the note one expects, which is such an important aspect of appoggiatura function.

Example 9

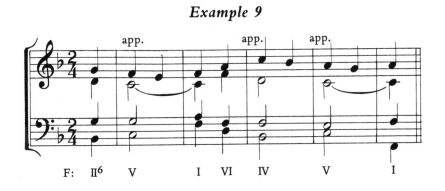

2. If the appoggiatura is approached by stepwise motion and resolved in the same direction as it was approached, some may wish to classify it as an accented passing tone. For the purpose of this book, the important distinction is that it is accented, thus functioning as an appoggiatura.

Suspension

A suspension is an accented dissonance that has grown out of a preceding consonance (by being held over) and will resolve by step (usually down) to another consonance (see Example 10). The function of the suspension is similar to the function of the appoggiatura: it delays the appearance of the note to which it resolves. The suspension must be prepared by the consonant introduction of the note that is to become dissonant on the following accented beat.

Example 10

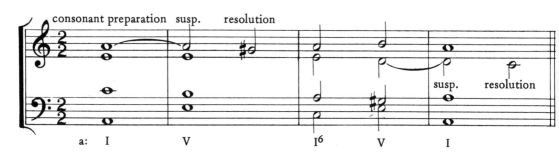

The tie is usually associated with the suspension, but a suspension may be said to occur without a tie. It is more common for suspensions to be resolved downward by step to the notes they displace, but upward resolution, particularly by half step, is not uncommon. Upward-resolving suspensions are sometimes called *retardations*. Finally, it is not customary to suspend a dissonance for a longer duration than that of its consonant preparation (see Example 11).

Example 11

Pedal Tone

A pedal tone is a note that is sustained in any voice, regardless of harmonic change. Its function is to inject a static element into the musical environment (see Example 12). A pedal tone will be consonant when it is introduced and consonant when it is terminated, but it must be dissonant with some tone (or tones) at some time while it is sounding. The pitch of the pedal tone is usually an important note in the key, such as a tonic or a dominant.

Example 12

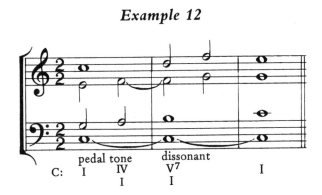

Échappée and Cambiata

The échappée, also known as the escape tone, is an unaccented nonchordal tone that leaves the melodic line by step and returns by leap. The cambiata is an unaccented nonchordal tone that leaves the line by leap and returns by step. The function of these nonharmonic tones is to ornament a basically stepwise line of melody.

Example 13

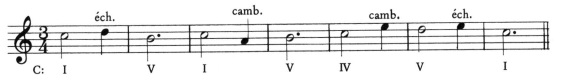

The normal interval of leap, in both cases, is that of a third. If wider leaps are involved, then the elaboration is not that of a basic stepwise line, but of notes that are themselves separated by a leap (see Example 14). The appropriate description, in such cases, is *extended* échappée, or *extended* cambiata.

Example 14

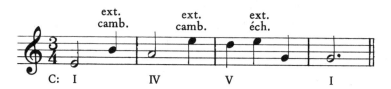

The échappée and cambiata are unusual among dissonances because they represent two of the rare occasions when dissonances may either be approached or left by leap. In almost all other cases, both the approach and the resolution of a dissonance is by step (or by holding the same pitch, as in the pedal tone).

Anticipation

The anticipation always occurs on the weak beat and may be chordal (if it is part of the chord sounding at the time it occurs), or, as is more common, it may be nonchordal. Its function is to sound in advance the tone that will occur on the following accented beat. The note sounding on the beat will always be a consonance.

Example 15

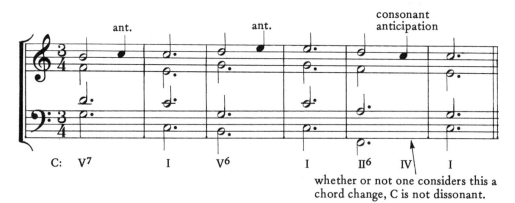

whether or not one considers this a
chord change, C is not dissonant.

Summary of Nonharmonic Tones

The first four types of nonharmonic tones listed in the chart represent the most common types. The others also occur frequently, but the beginning student is cautioned to use the less common varieties sparingly for the present. The first two, the passing tone and the neighbor note, are relatively easy to employ and should now be used wherever practical. A gradual facility in the use of appoggiaturas and suspensions should be acquired.

Nonharmonic Tones	
Unaccented	*Accented*
1. Passing tone 2. Neighbor note 5. Pedal tone 6. Échappée and cambiata 7. Anticipation	 3. Appoggiatura 4. Suspension 5. Pedal tone

It is wise to be cautious in the use of nonharmonic tones, since their function must always be clear. Of prime importance is the achievement of a more graceful or more interesting melodic line. A general rule should be: *Never overburden the musical texture with a great many nonharmonic tones.*

Nonharmonic tones are closely involved with establishing the underlying rhythmic movement of a musical composition. For any given piece, the basic unit of movement may be quarter notes, eighth notes, half notes, or some other less common note value. This movement is the sum of the rhythmic movements of each individual voice part and is called *composite rhythm*. It is generally sustained throughout a short piece or a short movement.

We can now return to the harmonization of the melody undertaken as a harmonization problem in the previous chapter (see Chapter 12, Example 6). Example 16 shows the same harmonization, but it has been elaborated by the use of nonharmonic tones in the alto, tenor, and bass parts. Note that the previous composite rhythm of quarter notes has now been changed to one of eighth notes and that the eighth-note movement is primarily sustained by nonharmonic tones.

Example 16

THE SIX-FOUR CHORD

Now that we have examined the function of a variety of unstable melodic notes (nonharmonic tones), it is possible to consider the use of an unstable combination of chord tones, the six-four chord, which is the second inversion of any triad. This inversion is unstable because it involves a dissonance that requires (as does all dissonance) careful approach and resolution.

In the six-four chord, the interval of a fourth is formed between one of the upper voices and the bass part. Such a formation has for hundreds of years been considered a dissonance. *Note:* Fourths that occur between upper voices only are not dissonant; however, any fourth that involves the bass note, as one of the two tones forming the interval, is dissonant.

Example 17

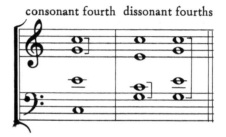

consonant fourth dissonant fourths

Accented Six-Fours

The most common second inversion is the tonic six-four; in most instances this is a chord that functions as a kind of appoggiatura to V. Like appoggiaturas, the tonic six-four must occur on an accented beat. In such a case the tonic six-four is considered to have a bass note on the dominant of the scale (functioning as the root of the dominant chord), with a note a fourth above it displacing the third of the dominant chord (as an appoggiatura) and with a note a sixth above the bass note similarly displacing the fifth of the dominant chord (as an appoggiatura). The resolution is shown in Example 18.

Example 18

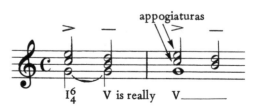

appogiaturas

I_4^6 V is really   V_____

In four parts it is customary to double the bass note of chords that present a double appoggiatura resolution in the upper voices. These accented six-four chords are called *appoggiatura six-fours*; however, when such a chord appears in a cadence formula, it is commonly called a *cadential six-four*, in recognition of its position within the phrase.

Example 19

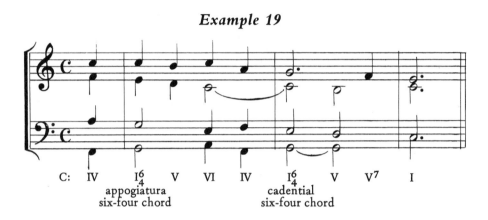

Unaccented Six-Fours

Six-four chords occurring on weak portions of the measure may similarly be classified according to nonharmonic functions. Because unaccented six-fours involve a dissonance with the bass, their treatment as a kind of nonharmonic chord insures a careful approach and resolution. Unlike the case of the accented appoggiatura six-four chord, we shall here refer to the movement of the bass (not the upper voices) in choosing labels for unaccented six-four chords. The most common types of unaccented six-fours are shown in Example 20.

Example 20

Passing six-four—
bass functions as
a passing tone

Auxiliary six-four—
bass functions as
an auxiliary

Pedal six-four—
bass functions as
a pedal tone.

C: I   V$_4^6$ I^6 I   V$_4^6$ I   I   IV$_4^6$ I

While the bass note is normally the note to double in accented six-fours, tonal doubling is recommended for unaccented six-fours. Of course, if the bass note is a tonal degree, it is a logical note to double.

Additional Uses of Six-Four Chords

An unaccented six-four may occur as an interpolation between two root-position triads in normal strong progression (see Example 21). In such a case, the upper voices generally move by step, but the bass is simply moving from root to root. In short, since the bass movement is unaffected by the interpolated six-four, the bass appears to have leaped away from the six-four chord. This is similar to the pedal six-four in its approach, but is different from the pedal six-four in that the bass does not become consonant before moving to the next note.

Example 21

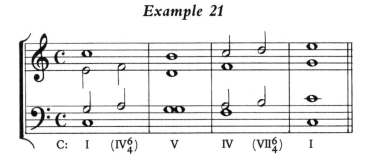

A six-four chord may also arise out of changing inversions of the triad, resulting in an arpeggiation of the bass line (see Example 22). Such a chord may occur on either an accented or an unaccented beat.

Example 22

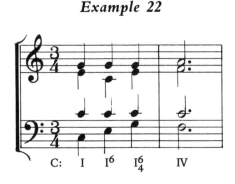

Unaccented six-four chords may be used at any point within the phrase, as long as they fit into a logical progression where their instability will not attract attention. The accented six-four (appoggiatura) most frequently occurs as a cadential six-four, coming between II and V or between IV and V in the introduction of a cadence. It is also possible to use appoggiatura six-fours on any accented beat elsewhere in the phrase.

Summary of the Use of Six-Four Chords

1. Never begin or end a phrase with a six-four chord. It is in no sense the equivalent of a root-position or a first-inversion triad.
2. Except in the case of the appoggiatura six-four chord (and also the six-four chord arising out of arpeggiation of the bass), it is not desirable to leap *to* the bass note of a six-four chord.
3. Never leap away from the bass of a six-four chord (except in the case of the unaccented interpolated six-four chord that occurs between two root-position triads).
4. Do not write two six-four chords in succession.
5. The more common harmonies that occur in second inversion are I, IV, and II.
6. Voice leading is usually stepwise in six-four usage; thus, doubling ought to arise out of voice leading. However, the bass note is normally the one to double in appoggiatura six-fours.

PERTAINING TO PART III EXAMPLES

1. Example Four offers many examples of passing tones and neighbor notes, several pedal tones, and a few suspensions and appoggiaturas. Note the use of the cadential six-four chord at each of the main cadences (measure 11, measure 21, and the final cadence).

2. Example Five is harmonically quite simple. It provides a good exercise in both the analysis of harmony and the use of nonharmonic tones.

3. Example Seven provides a good analysis exercise, with clear use of nonharmonic tones and consistent use of cadential six-four chords.

EXERCISES

1. Realize the following figured basses in four parts. Identify each six-four chord by its functional type and label each. Tastefully add a few nonharmonic tones if you feel the harmonization would be improved. Use passing tones and auxiliaries as a first choice. Add Roman numerals before you begin.

2. Make four-part harmonizations of the following soprano melodies, using some of the melodic notes as the nonharmonic tones implied by the melodies. Before beginning each harmonization, analyze the melody carefully to determine probable nonharmonic tones. If six-four chords are used, indicate the functional type of each. Add a complete harmonic analysis with Roman numerals and Arabic numbers.

3. Elaborate the following melody by using many nonharmonic tones (passing tones, auxiliaries, anticipations appoggiaturas, and suspensions, etc.) so that the composite rhythm made up of half notes will be increased to a composite rhythm of quarter notes. Remember that leaps of a third can be filled in by passing tones, that repeated notes can be elaborated by auxiliaries, and that stepwise movement can be decorated by anticipations. A leap of a fourth can be filled in by double passing tones, an elaboration that, in this context, would involve the use of eighth notes. Do *not* elaborate the final note of each phrase.

CHAPTER 14

Common-Chord Modulation

Modulation is the process of changing key. It is a process that takes place in nearly all tonal music, except in some very short pieces.

In the eighteenth and most of the nineteenth centuries a preference was shown for modulations that moved to closely related keys. This preference resulted in a large degree of overlap in the pitch content of the keys involved. Closely related keys are harmonically easy to get to and easy to return from—an important point, since compositions from this period almost always begin and end in the same key.

A great many modulations are clear-cut, leaving no doubt in the listener's mind about whether a modulation has actually taken place. However, transitory changes of key frequently occur; and there can be considerable doubt, in such cases, about whether a modulation has actually taken place or not. Transitory changes of key will be taken up in the next chapter; for the present, the discussion will be centered on unambiguous common-chord modulations.

Before a modulation can actually take place, three stages must have been accomplished. First, the initial key must be established. It is not until this has been done that it is possible to modulate to another key. Second, a harmonic area must be entered that provides material common to both keys. (For example, the triad ACE is III in F and II in G.) Third, a new key must be established. This is best done by having the music arrive at a well-defined cadence, a cadence that serves to confirm the new key.

PIVOT CHORDS

Because of the overlap between the harmonic material of closely related keys, it is usual to choose a chord common to both keys that can serve as a pivotal area leading out of one and into another. Such a chord is called a *pivot chord*. Example 1 explores the possibilities for finding a pivot chord between major keys that are somewhat closely related in terms of key signatures. The example shows that there are four chords in common between major keys whose signatures have a difference of only one chromatic alteration; there are two chords in common between major keys whose signatures have a difference of two chromatic alterations; and there are no chords in common between major keys that have a difference of more than two chromatic alterations.[1]

Example 1

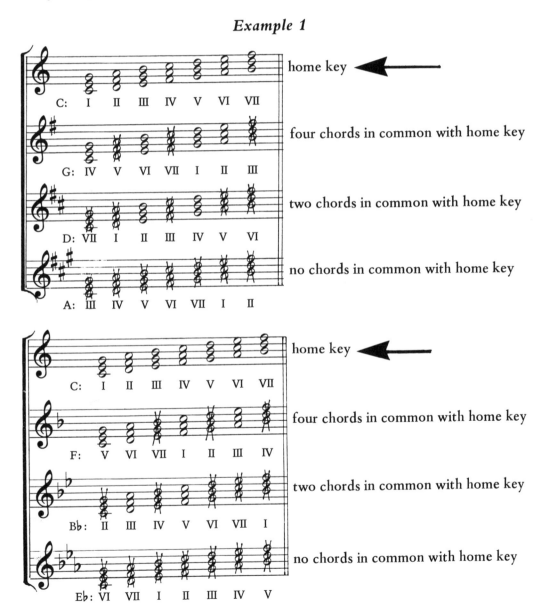

home key ◄───

C: I   II   III   IV   V   VI   VII

four chords in common with home key

G: IV   V   VI   VII   I   II   III

two chords in common with home key

D: VII   I   II   III   IV   V   VI

no chords in common with home key

A: III   IV   V   VI   VII   I   II

home key ◄───

C: I   II   III   IV   V   VI   VII

four chords in common with home key

F: V   VI   VII   I   II   III   IV

two chords in common with home key

Bb: II   III   IV   V   VI   VII   I

no chords in common with home key

Eb: VI   VII   I   II   III   IV   V

1.   With the exception of secondary dominants and certain chromatically altered (nondiatonic) chords that will be discussed in the final three chapters.

It is also interesting to note that the key of the *relative minor* shares four chords (in the harmonic form) with the home key of C major and that the *parallel minor* shares only two.

Example 2

CONFIRMING THE NEW KEY

It is extremely important to realize that it is necessary to confirm the new key *as soon as possible* by using chords or notes that do not occur in the old key as well. Example 3 presents two progressions, the first of which is a true modulation from the key of C major to the key of F major. The second progression appears to depict the same modulation, but because the new key has not been confirmed by a progression that could not occur in the old key, no modulation has taken place.

Example 3

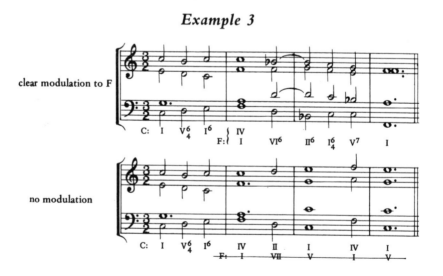

In analyzing music (melodies or compositions), the sudden appearance of chromatic alterations may indicate that a modulation is taking place (chromatic alterations may also only indicate the use of chromatically altered chords, which will be discussed in subsequent chapters). In order to determine whether or not a modulation has taken place, one should look for a cadence area where the new key has been confirmed and then work backward to the point of the first indication of the chromatic alteration (and subsequent harmonic progression) that would suggest the new key. The chord immediately preceding the chromatic alteration will likely be the pivot chord between the two keys.

Example 4

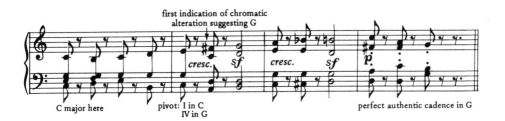

It is a fact that many musical compositions may present the analyst with the problem of deciding whether a modulation has really occurred or not. The main ambiguity in such cases arises out of the use of secondary dominants (the material of the next chapter). However, while the concept of three clear-cut areas (old key, pivot chord, new key) is of considerable help in arriving at a decision, there is no substitute for the confirmation that can be provided by the well-trained ear. Musicians must continually strive to improve their ability to hear musical functions such as modulations, for the musician's ear is the most reliable instrument for measuring the effect of any passage of music.

Surprisingly, a pivot chord that is V in the new key may sometimes prove ineffective as a pivot chord. This is because the chord following it may possibly sound too abrupt, thereby thwarting both the second and the third stages of a modulation.

A change from a major key to its parallel minor seems, at first glance, to be a remote possibility since (in the harmonic form) only the dominant triad and VII are held in common. Moreover, such a change is not considered a true modulation because the key center remains the same (C) in both cases. Instead, it is a change of mode. Nevertheless, movement between a major key and its parallel minor key is easily achieved, not by the use of a pivot chord, but by the direct process of "mixing" the modes, a process of freely borrowing chords from one mode to be used in the other. Since the third and sixth scale degrees are the modal degrees, such triads as VI, IV, III, and II, which contain these scale degrees, are quite suitable to begin a passage that will be changing to the parallel mode. More will be said about modal mixture in Chapter 17.

PERTAINING TO PART III EXAMPLES

1. In Example Three, according to some analysts,[2] a modulation from the key of C to the key of G exists from measures 5 to 10. While the visual evidence would seem to confirm this claim, an argument could be made that the actual sound of the music in those measures is more appropriately heard as an emphasis of the dominant, still within the key of C.

2. Although Example Eight involves a change of key, the passages in each key are clearly separated. Nonetheless, the relativity of the two keys (f minor and A flat major) does provide an easy common-chord link.

3. Example Nine involves a change of emphasis from B flat major to F major, and from c minor back to B flat major. The relation between F major and c minor involves a mixture of major-minor modes.

4. Note also the modulation in Example Four from C to G and back to C.

5. In Example Eighteen we find an interesting modulation from G to D, involving much treatment of D as a dominant within the key of G as a preparation for what is in measure 19 a somewhat unexpected change to D as a tonic.

6. Example Six provides a straightforward modulation from tonic to dominant, and back to tonic.

7. Example Fourteen provides a more complicated exercise in modulatory practice.

EXERCISES

1. Following Example 1 as a model, construct triads on every degree of the scale in each of the following keys:

   E major, A major, B major, D major; c sharp minor, f sharp minor

   Use the harmonic form of the minor. Considering E major to be the home key, find out which chords of the other keys are common (could serve as pivots) with the chords of E major.

2. Harmonize the following bass lines in four parts. Select an appropriate pivot chord for the change of key where the brace is indicated. A few nonharmonic tones will make the assignment more musical.

---

2. Walter Piston, *Principles of Harmonic Analysis* (Boston: E. C. Schirmer, 1933), pp. 54 and 55.

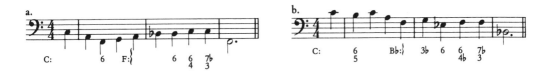

3. Make a four-part harmonization of each of the following bass and soprano melodies, modulating as indicated.

4. Make a four-part harmonization of the following soprano melodies, modulating to the appropriate keys in each case.

CHAPTER 15

Secondary
Dominants

Up to this point, we have only encountered chromatic alterations in the varying forms of the minor scale and in the process of modulation. Now the range of harmonic resources can be widened significantly by the use of dominant chords of other keys than the home key. Although these dominant chords do expand the resources of the given key by the introduction of chromatic alterations that are appropriate to other keys, they do not result in full-fledged modulations. Moreover, rather than weakening the tonality by the introduction of notes out of the key, these borrowed chords actually serve to underscore the strength of the tonality.

The fact is that any major or minor triad, on any degree of the scale, may be approached by its own dominant chord without weakening the key at hand. The result is a momentary V–I progression that is appropriate to another key, but is so transitory (actually the dominant is the only chord out of the key) that the potential for modulation is not realized.

The construction of *secondary dominants* is not difficult if one remembers that these chords must contain a leading tone. The leading tone of any secondary dominant (or any dominant, for that matter) is the third of the triad. In most cases (exceptions will be discussed later) the leading tone of the secondary dominant will be easy to identify because it will be chromatically raised by a half step. Remember that in each secondary-dominant progression the leading tone is momentarily that of the key of the chord to which the secondary dominant is moving or resolving. It is *not* the leading tone of the overall key. Thus, each secondary dominant resolves to its own tonic in exactly the same way that any ordinary dominant resolves to its tonic. Moreover, the addition of a seventh to the secondary-dominant triad will enhance the dominant feeling of the chord.

STEPS IN THE USE OF SECONDARY DOMINANTS

1. Identify the root of the triad to which the secondary dominant should resolve. A half step below that root is its leading tone (the third of the secondary-dominant triad).
2. Build a major triad containing that leading tone as its third (the root is a major third below, the fifth is a minor third above).
3. Resolve the triad you have built in the same manner as any dominant-to-tonic progression. Secondary dominants may be used in all inversions, and they function just like ordinary dominants. The main requirement is that they have the ability to resolve to chords within the key of the piece that can stand as their momentary tonics (major or minor).

Example 1

C: V of II (7)   II   V of III (7)   III   V⁷ of IV   IV   V of V   V   V of VI   VI

note here that the secondary leading tone (E) does not have to be raised. Therefore the addition of the seventh is crucial to the perception of the chord as a dominant, rather than the I chord in C major.

Chromatic Alteration

Most secondary dominants (without the added seventh) have only one chromatic alteration, the third of the triad, which is in fact the leading tone of the secondary dominant.

Only V of IV in major keys, and V of III and V of VI in the harmonic scale of minor keys, do not have such chromatically raised leading tones. Therefore, in order to clarify the dominant function of these chords, the addition of a seventh is appropriate (see Example 2).

Example 2

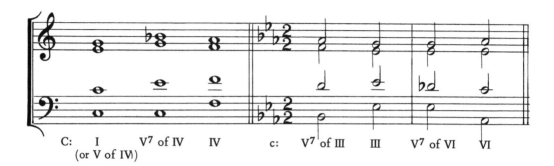

C: I   V⁷ of IV   IV   c: V⁷ of III   III   V⁷ of VI   VI
   (or V of IV)

In major keys V of III has two chromatically raised degrees (the fifth also being raised to avoid the tritone dissonance with the root).

Example 3

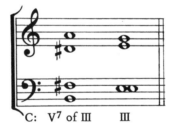

C: V⁷ of III   III

Cross-Relation

Now that chromatic alteration has been introduced, it is necessary to consider a problem growing out of the use of accidentals: the cross-relation. A cross-relation occurs when an unaltered note in any chord is followed by the chromatically altered version of that same note *in a different voice part.* (The reverse is also a cross-relation, as when an altered tone is followed by the unaltered form of that same note in a different voice.) The cross-relation has been treated with care by composers because of the important melodic forces that are involved. One type of cross-relation we have already encountered is found in the ascending and descending forms of the melodic minor scale (see Example 4). Here, as in all cases, the justification of the cross relation is simply the logic of good voice leading.

Example 4

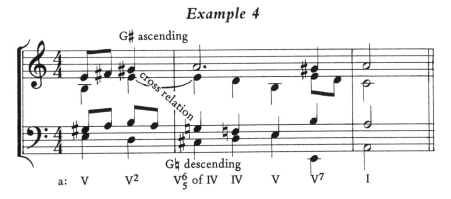

The examination of actual music will show that a few composers, Henry Purcell for example, have been somewhat daring in their use of cross-relations. However, composers have commonly used cross-relations only when the melodic voice leading involves stepwise motion to and from the altered note.

Example 5

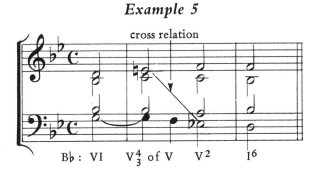

Another cross-relation composers have found to be generally acceptable is that which occurs when the altered degree is at the same pitch (even though in a different voice part) as would have been the case if only a single voice part were involved. Example 6 shows an A sharp adjacent to an A natural; even though two voices are involved, it is clear to the listener that the A sharp comes from the A natural and progresses to the B.

Example 6

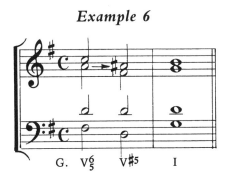

The following principle can now be stated: *Any chromatic progression ought to occur in a single voice part, unless the melodic direction of the voice leading is absolutely clear.*

Example 7

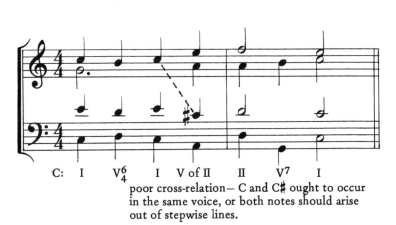

C: I   V$^6_4$ I   V of II   II   V^7 I

poor cross-relation— C and C♯ ought to occur in the same voice, or both notes should arise out of stepwise lines.

DECEPTIVE AND IRREGULAR RESOLUTION OF SECONDARY DOMINANTS

The regular resolution of any dominant chord or secondary-dominant chord involves root movement up a fourth (or down a fifth). A less common progression that has already been discussed is the V–VI progression. The resolution of this progression is root up a second, and it is generally thought of as a deceptive resolution of a dominant chord.

The same principles may be applied to secondary dominants. They may resolve up a second if provision is made for proper treatment of all tendency tones (at this point, the leading tone and the seventh) and if the chords to which they resolve are diatonic within the key of the piece. A clear relationship to the overall key of the piece is important in avoiding a progression that will seem like a modulation, assuming that a modulation is not desired at that point.

We remember that the triad of VI (in the V–VI progression) necessarily includes a doubled third degree. The same holds true in deceptive resolutions of secondary dominants, regardless of the fact that the doublings that result may not necessarily be tonal (see Example 8). However, if the chord of resolution is a dominant itself, one would not double the leading tone in that chord.

Example 8

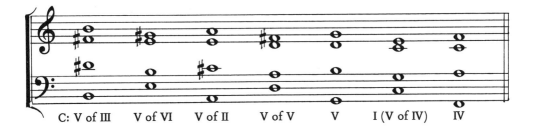

Sequence of Dominants

Another common irregular resolution of secondary-dominant harmonies occurs in the so-called sequence of dominants around the circle of fifths. In this case, the secondary dominant does not resolve to the chord that normally stands as its tonic (often a minor triad); instead, it resolves to a major triad built on that same root, which, in turn, functions as another dominant (either a secondary dominant or an ordinary dominant). Such a sequence of dominants can continue completely around the circle of fifths; however, if one wishes to use such a sequence without leaving the key (modulating), the chain of dominants shown in Example 9 is possible.

Example 9

It is possible to use this same sequence with an added seventh for each dominant chord. The effect is compelling, because the added seventh supplies more urgency to the tendency of the chords to progress one to another. The seventh may be added as a passing tone, as Example 10 shows.

Example 10

It is also possible to create the sequence illustrated in Example 10 by moving directly from one dominant seventh to the next dominant seventh (avoiding the dominant triad without the added seventh). In such a case (Example 11), the leading tone of one dominant seventh moves directly downward by half step to the seventh of the next dominant.

Example 11

This would appear to present a new possibility for leading-tone treatment: that of moving down by half step when a sequence of dominant sevenths (around the circle of fifths) is involved. Of course, we can see by comparing Example 11 with Example 10 that this downward resolution has really evolved from normal voice leading by a process of contraction.

Another common irregular resolution of dominant and secondary-dominant harmony is the progression V–IV₆.

Example 12

PERTAINING TO PART III EXAMPLES

Secondary dominants are such a common aspect of eighteenth- and nineteenth-century music that examples are easily found.

1. Example Ten is a particularly fruitful example in which secondary dominants occur in rapid succession.

2. Example Eighteen provides several instances of V of V, as well as other secondary dominants.

3. Example Twelve provides an unusual resolution of a secondary dominant in measure 8.

4. Example Six illustrates the downward resolution (contraction) of the leeding tone by half step in measures 1–2, 4–5, and 9.

5. Look again at Example Three (as you did in Chapter 14). This time, instead of considering measures 5 to 10 to be a modulation from C major to G major, analyze those measures so that no modulation occurs and all of the dominants of G are felt to be V of V chords. Compare that analysis with the one suggested at the end of the previous chapter to see whether you think the music actually modulates or whether a secondary-dominant emphasis is all that is involved. Find reasons to support your decision.

EXERCISES

1. In four-part harmony, with a chord to precede each resolution, resolve V₇ of II, V₇ of III, and V₇ of VI to each of their respective tonics (regular resolution). Do this in each of the following keys:

A flat major	g minor
E major	c minor
B flat major	f sharp minor
D major	b minor

2. In four-part harmony, with a chord to precede each resolution, resolve V₇ to four different chords (irregular resolutions) in the same keys indicated in exercise 1 above.

3. Realize the following figured bass in four parts; be sure to add a Roman numeral analysis.

4. Make a four-part harmonization of the following basses, using secondary dominants wherever they might be appropriate. Label chords and inversions with Roman numerals and Arabic numbers.

5. Make a four-part harmonization of the following soprano melodies, using secondary dominants as appropriate. Label each chord.

CHAPTER 16

Diminished Sevenths and Other Dominant Dissonance

We have already gone beyond simple triadic harmony by adding sevenths to triads in the formation of dominant and nondominant seventh chords. The next step is to add still more thirds above the chordal structures to form such higher dissonances as ninth chords, elevenths, or thirteenths. Because of the importance of dominant harmony, such formations are often associated with dominant chords; however, they can be formed with any chord, whether it is a dominant or not.

In each case, the ninth, eleventh, or thirteenth is treated like a nonharmonic tone (usually an appoggiatura), and can be most simply and logically understood in this manner. In four-part writing it is necessary to omit a tone for each higher tone (above the seventh) that is added. As we have seen before, the fifth of the triad is frequently omitted whenever doubling or the addition of other tones displaces a note of the chord. Of course, an appoggiatura usually displaces the tone of the triad to which it resolves, as the appoggiatura resolution of V_9, V_{11}, and V_{13} in Example 1 shows.

Example 1

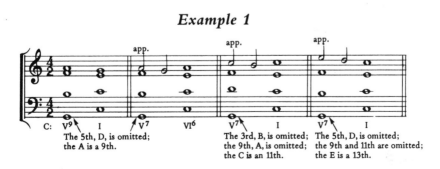

The 5th, D, is omitted; the A is a 9th.

The 3rd, B, is omitted; the 9th, A, is omitted; the C is an 11th.

The 5th, D, is omitted; the 9th and 11th are omitted; the E is a 13th.

We have, in previous chapters, studied the following dominant chords:

Example 2

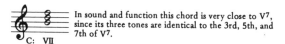

In sound and function this chord is very close to V⁷, since its three tones are identical to the 3rd, 5th, and 7th of V⁷.

In our study of seventh chords we postponed a consideration of dominant chords built upon the leading tone as a root. Because such chords function as higher dominant dissonances, we shall begin this chapter with a study of seventh chords that are built on the leading tone. The two usual forms are the half-diminished chord and the diminished seventh chord.

Example 3

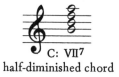

half-diminished chord

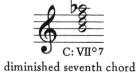

diminished seventh chord

The half-diminished chord is a diatonic seventh chord (in major keys) built upon the leading tone of the scale, and it is dominant in function.[1] The diminished seventh chord, like the half-diminished chord, is dominant in function, and it is also a seventh chord built on the leading tone of the scale. It is indicated with a degree sign (the small circle), which shows that its seventh is a diminished seventh above the root. In both of these chords the seventh resolves down by step, in the manner of all sevenths. If the other notes of the chord remain unchanged, while the seventh resolves down by step (or half step), one can easily see that the seventh in this case is functioning as an appoggiatura displacing the root of V_5^6 (the chord into which the appoggiatura resolves). This kind of resolution (shown in Example 4) can be called a nonchordal resolution, and it underscores the dominant function of these chords.

---

1. Some theorists identify this chord as an incomplete ninth chord in which the uppermost tone is heard as a ninth above the implied (nonexistent) root of V. The half-diminished chord is indicated by such theorists as V°₉, and the diminished seventh as V°₉♭.

Example 4

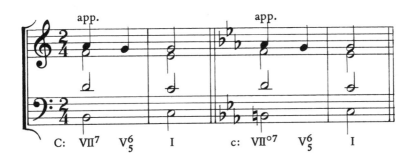

THE DIMINISHED SEVENTH CHORD

The more common of these two chords is the diminished seventh chord, and it can be most directly described as VII₇ as it occurs in the harmonic minor scale. However, it is common in both the major and minor modes; and when it occurs in the major mode, it is a chromatically altered chord because its seventh is lowered to create the diminished seventh above the root. It is close in appearance to the dominant seventh in first inversion, except that the root of V_5^6 has been replaced by the tone that is a diminished seventh above the leading tone.

In the root position of the diminished seventh chord the leading tone is the lowest note; above that root are superposed three tones, each of which is separated from its adjacent tone by the interval of a minor third. Inversions are numbered analytically exactly like inversions of other four-note chords, while VII⁰ remains an unvarying indicator that the chord (regardless of its inversion) is a diminished seventh chord.

Example 5

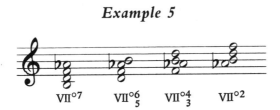

The sound of a diminished seventh chord is basically an intensification of dominant harmony. The addition of the diminished seventh interval to the triad of VII has increased the number of tendency tones so that at least three of the four tones of the chord have a prescribed resolution: leading tone up, seventh and fifth down. (These tones are the same as leading tone, seventh, and ninth above an implied dominant root, and the direction of resolution is the same.)

Because the chord contains two tritones, it is also common to double the third in the chord of resolution, even though it may be a modal degree (see Example 6a). This doubling permits the resolution of both tritone intervals (A4 expanding to a sixth, or d5 contracting to a third). (If, however, the chord of resolution is a dominant chord—as in the resolution VII$_7^9$ of V–V—one would not resolve into a doubled leading tone; see Example 7c.) If the tritone within the inner voices is an augmented fourth, it is possible for it to resolve to a perfect fourth (see Example 6b); however, if the interval is a diminished fifth, it is less common to permit a resolution to a perfect fifth (see Example 6c).

Example 6

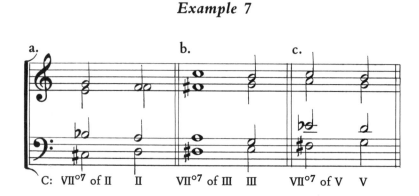

The diminished seventh chord may be used with equal facility in either major or minor keys, and it is an easy chord with which to begin a passage in which a mixture of modes may be involved. As mentioned earlier, the diminished seventh chord is an unaltered chord in the harmonic minor scale, but is a chromatically altered chord in the major scale.

Diminished sevenths, like other dominant chords, may be used as secondary dominants, provided the resolution is to the chord that stands as its tonic.

Example 7

The diminished seventh is a chord of many ambiguities (since its four tones divide the octave into equal parts), which enables it to serve easily as a pivot chord in modulations. Since the interval between any two of its adjacent tones is the same (minor third in every instance) and no perfect fifth is possible between any two notes of the chord, it is possible (by means of enharmonic respelling) for the diminished seventh chord to have a variety of interpretations (because exactly the same pitches are sounding), each of which depends on its resolution (see Example 8).

Example 8

Because of the ambiguity of the diminished seventh chord, an irregular resolution would not be meaningful. The chromatic alterations indicate the direction each note should move in its resolution. Example 9 shows that VII$^\circ_7$ has no deceptive resolution because the same chord, by enharmonic respelling, is actually the dominant of the relative minor.

Example 9

Example 10 shows what appears, in light of the foregoing discussion, to be an irregular use.

Example 10

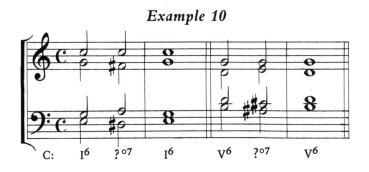

In these resolutions (Example 10) there is not the usual dominant-to-tonic resolution, but rather an embellishment of the chords to which they resolve. A voice-leading function is involved because these chords result from a coincidence of nonharmonic tones (neighbor notes, in the example shown). In this case, the two diminished seventh chords could be analyzed as $\sharp II_7^{\circ}$ and $\sharp VI_7^{\circ}$ (indicating that they are diminished sevenths whose roots are the raised second and the raised sixth degrees of the scale, without dominant function). To consider them to be VII_7° of III and VII_7° of VII, resolving irregularly, seems less correct because the complexity of the situation calls for a simple and unambiguous interpretation.

THE HALF-DIMINISHED CHORD

The half-diminished chord is indicated as VII_7. It occurs as an unaltered chord in the major scale, but it does not usually occur in minor keys because the seventh (which is the sixth degree of the scale) resolves down. In a minor key it would involve the raised sixth and would have to ascend according to the expectation of the melodic form of the minor scale. It is close in appearance to the dominant seventh in first inversion, except that the root of V_5^6 has been replaced by the tone that is a minor seventh above the leading tone. Example 11 shows the root position and inversions of the half-diminished chord.

Example 11

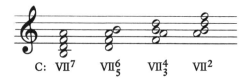

$$C: \quad VII^7 \qquad VII_5^6 \qquad VII_3^4 \qquad VII^2$$

Like the diminished seventh chord, the half-diminished chord represents an intensification of dominant sound. It may be used where any dominant might have been used in a major key, and it may be used as a secondary dominant in both the major and the minor modes. The resolution of this chord is quite similar to that of the diminished seventh chord: leading tone up, seventh and fifth down. Because the chord contains a perfect fifth (or perfect fourth in inversion), there is a danger of parallel fifths in forming the resolution. These, of course, ought to be avoided, regardless of the doubling that results in the chord of resolution. However, in secondary dominant usage (VII_7 of V to V) one would not resolve into a doubled leading tone.

Example 12

incorrect   correct   correct

F: VII^7 I VII^7 I VII^7 of V   V

Unlike the diminished seventh chord, the half-diminished chord does not have identical distance between adjacent tones in every case; and its tones do not divide the octave into equal parts. Therefore, it is not the ambiguous chord that the diminished seventh is, and its limitations as a pivot chord are clear. It is ambiguous only with II_7 in the key of the relative minor.

Example 13

G: VII^7 e: II^7

Irregular resolutions are possible for the half-diminished chord, as long as proper care is taken to resolve tendency tones and provided the voice leading is satisfactory. While a suitable use of irregular resolutions requires experimenting, the following comments are offered as a guide (also see Example 14).

VII_7–II   Weak; all of the tones of II are also in VII_7.
VII_7–III   Strong; root up a fourth.
VII_7–IV_4^6 Strong; IV_4^6 will likely resolve to I in deferred resolution.
VII_7–VI_6 Strong; sounds like a resolution to I with an added sixth.

Example 14

weak   strong   strong   strong   regular

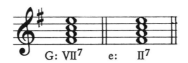

C: VII^7 II VII^7 III VII^7 IV_4^6 VII^7 VI^6 VII^7 I

THE DOMINANT NINTH

As its name implies, the dominant ninth is a dominant chord with a tone a major or a minor ninth above the root. Since there are five tones in such a chord (see Example 17) and since the study of harmony is concerned with four melodic lines, the fifth of the chord is often omitted (see Example 15). This is because it is not a tendency tone and because it is less functionally important than the other tones that must be resolved.

Example 15

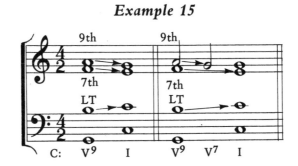

The ninth as a melodic tone is likely to function as an appoggiatura. Its resolution may be to its root before the chord changes, or the resolution may come at the same moment as the chord changes. It may also occur as a passing tone or as a neighbor note.

Example 16

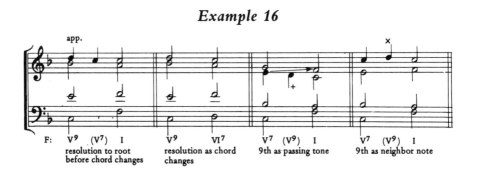

The dominant ninth chord occurs most commonly in root position. Since the note to which it resolves is also present in the chord (the root), it is desirable to have as much distance as possible between the ninth and the root. Moreover, if the chord were inverted, it would present a somewhat unstable sound because in its complete five-part state it combines all the tones of the supertonic triad as well as the dominant triad. A general rule for the use of ninth chords: *Always keep the ninth more than an octave above the root.*

Example 17

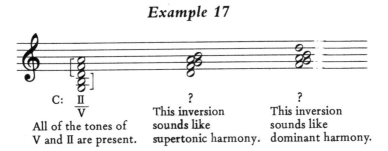

C: II
    —
    V

All of the tones of   ?   ?
V and II are present.   This inversion   This inversion
                   sounds like   sounds like
                   supertonic harmony. dominant harmony.

The dominant ninth chord occurs as either a major ninth or a minor ninth chord. The minor ninth may be used easily in either the major or the minor mode (and is unaltered if it occurs in the harmonic minor scale); but the major ninth is generally used in the major mode only because the melodic minor scale prohibits normal resolution (as with the half-diminished chord), unless a mixture of modes is involved.

In resolving the dominant ninth, the leading tone moves up; the seventh and the ninth move down; and the root is free to move where the progression takes it. The dominant ninth resolves to any chord to which any dominant would resolve, so long as proper resolution of the ninth, as a tendency tone, is provided for. The chord is not generally effective as a pivot chord in modulations because of its strong dominant character and its lack of functional ambiguities.

PERTAINING TO PART III EXAMPLES

1. Example Fifteen presents the diminished seventh as a dominant or as a secondary dominant in measures 5, 6, 10, 11, 12, and in the repetition of the same material; measures 13, 14, 15, and 16 present diminished seventh arpeggiation and enharmonic respelling; in measures 3 and 15 there is a half-diminished chord.

2. Example Seventeen contains many diminished sevenths and secondary dominants.

3. Example Thirteen contains two long diminished seventh arpeggios (measures 15 and 17).

4. Example Nine contains examples of diminished seventh chords in measures 6, 12, 13, and 24.

5. Example Fourteen provides an example of a complete minor ninth chord in measure 14, and a complete major ninth chord in measure 22.

EXERCISES

1. In four-part harmony, with a chord to precede the resolution, resolve the following diminished seventh chord to as many different chords as possible (show at least four resolutions). This will require enharmonic respelling of the chord when it is interpreted in different keys.

2. Harmonize the following bass and soprano lines in four parts, using diminished seventh chords where it is marked *. Label each chord using Roman numerals and Arabic numbers.

3. Harmonize the following soprano in four parts, using as many diminished seventh chords as is musically satisfactory. Label chords and inversions with appropriate numerals.

4.   Realize the following figured basses in four parts. Label all chords and
     inversions.

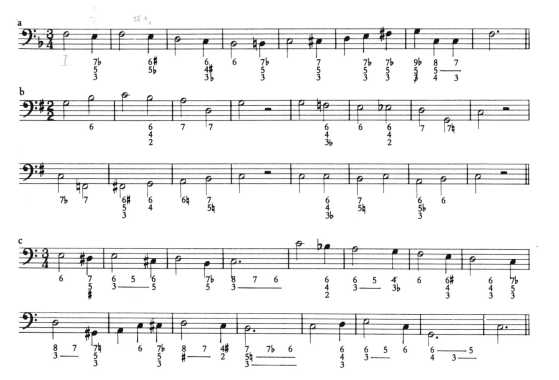

CHAPTER 17

Altered Chords: Neapolitan and Augmented Sixths

THE NEAPOLITAN SIXTH CHORD

The Neapolitan sixth chord is a major triad, generally used in first inversion, with a root that is the lowered second degree of the scale (♭II₆). The use of the word "Neapolitan" incorrectly implies a national connotation; however, the fact that the chord usually occurs in first inversion justifies the rest of its name.

It is a chord that is closer to the minor mode than to the major mode because two of its three tones belong to the minor scale. Moreover, in major keys two of its three tones are altered.

Example 1

Only F is in the key of C major.

F and A♭ are in the key of c minor.

C: ♭II⁶   c: ♭II⁶

150

The third of the triad is doubled in normal use, partly because that is a tonal degree, but more importantly because in major keys that is the only unaltered note of the triad. Most often, bII_6 resolves to V or to I^6_4 (which then leads into V). Another relatively frequent resolution is to IV.

Example 2

In the first resolution of Example 2, the melodic movement by the interval of a diminished third (a dissonant interval) is permitted, and so also is the cross-relation that occurs between the Neapolitan root and the fifth of the dominant triad. The other resolutions of the Neapolitan sixths in the example do not require any special dispensations.

Any approach to bII_6 that involves good voice leading is likely to be successful, but it is always desirable to consider as many options as possible and to experiment with them. In minor keys VI is an excellent approach because VI is also V of bII; IV or I are both good choices also. Since the Neapolitan sixth chord is an alteration of the supertonic triad, II is also likely to provide a satisfactory approach. To approach from V_7 of bII expands the secondary dominants available and is a more urgent approach than VI (without the added seventh). It is particularly useful in major keys.

Example 3

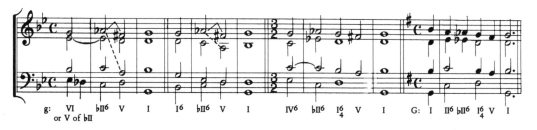

In the resolutions to V (Example 3), note again the cross-relation and the diminished third melodic leap. In the resolutions to I^6_4, note the parallel fourths between soprano and alto. Of course, these are correct; however, if these two voices had been reversed, parallel fifths would have resulted, and this would not have been as acceptable.

The Neapolitan sixth is often used as a supertonic variant in cadence formulas: $\flat II_6 - I_4^6 - V - I$ (as shown in the third and fourth parts of Example 3). However, it may be used anywhere within the phrase, provided the context is of a similarly colorful nature. It is also often used as an alternative to the diminished triad, II_3^6 in minor.

The Neapolitan sixth may function as a pivot chord because it can be reinterpreted as another major triad (in another key) in first inversion.

Example 4

$$c: \quad \flat II^6 = D\flat: I^6$$
$$G\flat: V^6$$
$$A\flat: IV^6$$
$$b\flat: III^6$$
$$f: VI^6$$

It may also occur in root position instead of first inversion, as in Example 5, especially if it moves to first inversion before resolving.

Example 5

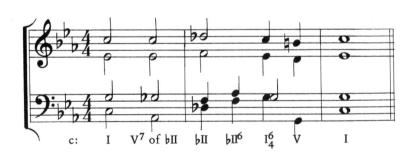

$$c: \quad I \quad V^7 \text{ of } \flat II \quad \flat II \quad \flat II^6 \quad I_4^6 \quad V \quad I$$

A secondary use of $\flat II_6$ is also possible, in which case it is used to elaborate (approach) a secondary dominant within the key. Example 6 illustrates the use of $\flat II_6$ of V. Note that this is really a mixing of the major and minor modes, because VI in the minor mode bears a Neapolitan relationship to V.

Example 6

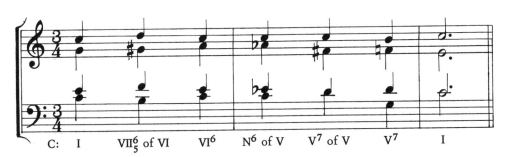

THE AUGMENTED SIXTH CHORD

The augmented sixth chord is basically a modification of subdominant or supertonic harmony, and its function is like a varied form of the dominant of the dominant (V_3^4 of V). The augmented sixth provides an excellent example of a contrapuntal chord that results from chromatic melodic movement. Although there are four common forms of the chord, it is the augmented sixth interval (contained in each of the four forms) that in and of itself urgently seeks resolution by expanding to the octave.

Example 7

The augmented 6th, A♭–F♯, expands to the G octave (the dominant of the key at hand).

The "fundamental" position (analogous to root position) for each augmented sixth chord has the lower tone of the augmented sixth interval in the bass voice, and the tones of the basic triad are derived from the minor form of the subdominant triad in first inversion. The root of IV₆ (from the minor mode) is then raised by half step, creating the augmented sixth interval with the bass.

Example 8

C:

1st step: IV⁶ from
the minor mode

C:

2nd step: raise the
root of IV, creating
augmented 6th

Although theorists have used both the Roman numerals IV or II (with appropriate Arabic numbers) to indicate the chord, the sound of the augmented sixth is controlled by the unique nature of the augmented sixth interval itself, rather than by a functional root.

Example 9 shows the four most common forms of the augmented sixth chord. The Roman numeral analysis of these chords suggests that the Italian and German augmented sixths function as variants of the subdominant. It should be noted, however, that the tritone C–F sharp suggests strongly that augmented sixths are varied forms of V_3^4 of V. In fact, the French form is really V_3^4 of V with a lowered fifth.

Example 9

common analysis symbols
for augmented sixth chords

C: IV#6 II#6/4 IV#6/b5 II#6/#4

Italian | French | German | dbly. Aug. 4th

Moreover, the Roman numeral analysis of the German form and of the form containing a doubly augmented fourth[1] suggests that there is a change of root between these two forms of the chord, from IV to II; however, the two chords have exactly the same sound, being enharmonically identical, and it is only through their resolution that a difference can be perceived.

The two common means of designating the different forms of the augmented sixth chord are shown in Example 9 (Roman numeral designation or traditional geographical designation). We recommend another designation

---

1. The chord containing the interval of the doubly augmented fourth has been called, somewhat less commonly, the "English Sixth."

as preferable—the use of the abbreviation "Aug." with the appropriate Arabic numbers—as a means of pointing out the significance of the augmented sixth interval in determining the harmonic personality of augmented sixth chords as a single grouping (see Example 10).

Example 10

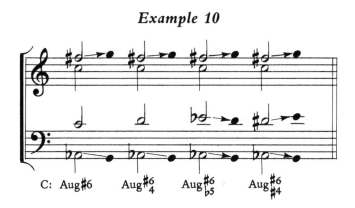

The stable element in the construction of these chords is the three-part "skeleton" of the subdominant triad from the minor mode, in first inversion. The root of that subdominant triad is then raised by half step. Finally, the fourth note is added, and it is the pitch of that fourth note that establishes which of the four types has been constructed.

The most frequent resolution of the augmented sixth chord is to V, V_7, or to I_4^6 (which most probably will then progress to V). The augmented sixth interval expands to the octave (which will be the dominant degree of the scale) by half steps, and the other voices will resolve by following the direction of chromatic alteration in each case.

Example 11

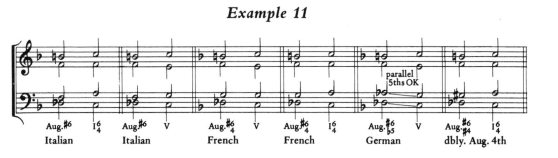

In approaching the augmented sixth chord in a harmonic progression (and in approaching any chromatically altered chord), one frequently uses an unaltered form of the triad or chord on which the altered chord is built. This would mean, in the case of the augmented sixth chord, an approach through

IV_6, II_4^6, or V_3^4 of V. Such an approach would make maximum use of the augmented sixth as a contrapuntal chord. It should be noted that the resolution of the German augmented sixth to the dominant triad naturally gives rise to parallel fifths (see Example 12). Composers have not generally avoided using these fifths unless they occur between soprano and bass. They most frequently occur between tenor and bass, and an example of Mozart's use of parallel fifths (in the resolution of the German sixth) can be seen in measures 13 and 14 of Example Eight, Part III.

Example 12

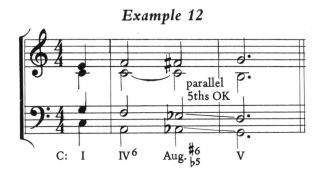

Augmented Sixth as Pivot Chord

In addition to its use as an intensification of subdominant or supertonic harmony, or to its use as a varied dominant of the dominant, the augmented sixth chord is an effective pivot chord in modulations between keys that are not closely related. The German form of the augmented sixth chord (as well as the form of the doubly augmented fourth) is enharmonically identical to the dominant seventh chord of the key a half step above the key in which the augmented sixth occurs. The lowest tone of the augmented sixth chord in its fundamental position (that is to say, the lower tone of the augmented sixth interval) is the same note as the root of the dominant seventh chord with which it is enharmonically identical. When one realizes that this dominant seventh may function as a secondary dominant as well as an ordinary dominant, the potential for modulation becomes apparent.

Example 13

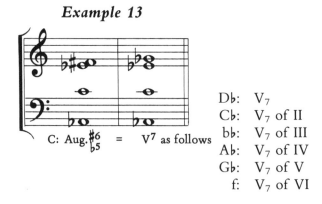

Although it is possible to use this chord in inversions (in which case the augmented sixth interval inverts to a diminished third), it is much more commonly found in fundamental position. There are many irregular uses of the augmented sixth, and the most common of these (shown in Example 14) is a secondary use, analogous to the use of secondary dominants.

Example 14

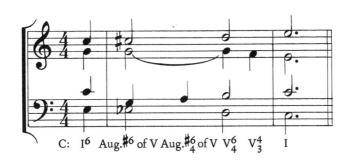

General Use of Augmented Sixths

Here are two rules for the use of augmented sixth chords:

1. Any major triad may be preceded by an augmented sixth chord whose lowest tone (in fundamental position) is one half step higher than the root of that major triad.
2. Any $^6_4$ chord may be preceded by an augmented sixth chord whose lowest tone (in fundamental position) is one half step higher than the bass note of that $^6_4$ chord.

Look at Example 14 for a demonstration of these rules.

ADDITIONAL ALTERATION

One frequently finds, within the context of a major key, the introduction of tones and chords from the minor scale. The reverse, the use of tones and chords from the major scale within the context of a minor key, is also possible. One of the more common instances of mixing the modes is the use of the raised third in the final tonic chord of a piece in a minor key. This is called a *Tièrce de Picardie* (*Picardy third*). It is different from other alterations only in that it does not function (resolve) in the context of the composition. Instead, it is a coloristic device for the final chord only.

Example 15

In discussing the Neapolitan sixth chord at the beginning of this chapter, we discovered that it is more closely related to the minor scale than to the major scale. Although its root (the lowered second degree of the scale) is altered in either mode, the fact that VI in the minor mode is its dominant and the fact that it involves the sixth degree of the minor scale as one of its tones explain why it is more commonly found in minor keys. Thus, the use of N_6 in major keys constitutes at least a mixture (melodically) of modes. The same can be said of the augmented sixth chord because of its relationship to the first inversion of the subdominant triad from the minor mode.

Among the more common forms of triads from the minor mode that appear in major keys are: I♭, IV♭, ♭VI (Neapolitan of V), and ♭VII.[1]

Example 16

---

1.   This calls attention to the notational importance of putting the accidentals on the correct side of the Roman numeral. ♭IV is quite a different matter than IV♭. ♭IV indicates a triad with a root which is the lowered 4th degree of the scale; IV♭ means that the 3rd of the subdominant triad is lowered.

Doubling the root in root-position chords is still an important principle. If one wishes to avoid an abrupt sound when introducing a modal mixture, it is important to employ careful voice leading. Doubling, then, becomes all the more a result of melodic line and the coincidence of available chord tones, rather than an attempt to double a particular note of a chord. Again, remember that it is not desirable to double a tone that forms a dissonance with another tone of the chord.

Example 17
A simple example of mixed modes

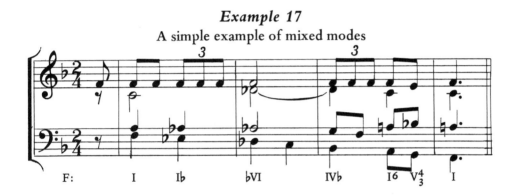

Another altered chord that is commonly used is the *augmented triad*. We have encountered it briefly before as III in the harmonic minor and as III in the ascending melodic minor forms, but it more commonly exists as an altered form of any major triad. Such alteration creates a contrapuntal force in which the altered note demands resolution. Passing-tone use of this chord is shown in Example 18. Any resolution that satisfies the upward drive of the raised fifth is acceptable.

Example 18

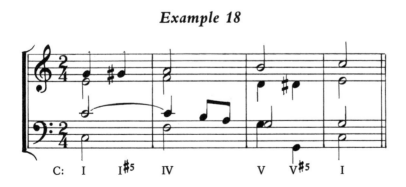

One occasionally encounters a variant of the dominant chord in which the fifth of the triad is flatted. Any resolution is possible that satisfies the directional tendencies of the lowered fifth degree and the leading tone.

Example 19

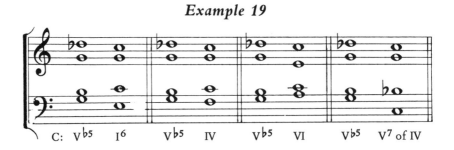

The inverted form of this chord, with seventh added, is not uncommon (see Example 20). It is clear that it can also be considered to be an irregular or secondary use of the augmented sixth chord.

Example 20

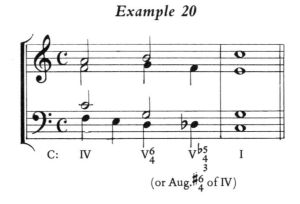

It is possible to devise other altered chords, using them according to the principle that an altered tone seeks resolution by step in the direction of its alteration. However, care in spelling is extremely important, as the false functional interpretation in the chord analysis in Example 21 will show.

Example 21

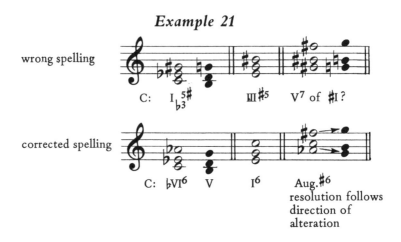

SUMMARY OF MODULATION BY ALTERED PIVOT CHORDS

While it is true that music of the eighteenth century and much of the nineteenth century presents a close relationship among the keys involved in any well-constructed musical composition, there are occasionally reasons for constructing modulations to remote keys. In such situations, the common-chord pivot is of no help, unless an extension of the principle is made to include secondary dominants.

Although secondary dominants do involve the introduction of chromatic alterations, they are not generally considered to be chromatically altered chords. They provide a kind of intermediary relationship between simple diatonic chords and the more specialized chromatic harmonies that may more appropriately be called altered chords. This is because secondary dominants serve to reinforce the tonal strength of the key in which they occur, on the one hand, and at the same time they extend the boundaries of tonality by introducing the more colorful sounds of accidentals.

The various enharmonic relationships of such chromatically altered chords as the diminished seventh, the Neapolitan sixth, and the augmented sixth have all been discussed. However, a tabular summary of these resources may be helpful.

Chord	Functions in old key as:	Functions in new key as:
Diminished seventh	VII°_7 or VII°_7 of _____	* VII°_7, or * VII°_7 of _____ * involves enharmonic respelling)
Neapolitan sixth	First inversion of any major triad	Neapolitan sixth
	Neapolitan sixth	First inversion of any major triad
Augmented sixth	V_7 or V_7 of _____	* augmented sixth
	augmented sixth	* V_7 or * V_7 of _____ * (involves enharmonic respelling)

Example 22 is an example of simple modulations to remote keys. Note that when enharmonic respelling is involved, the spelling is appropriate for the new key, so that the resolutions of the various tendency tones are clear.

Example 22

PERTAINING TO PART III EXAMPLES

1. *Neapolitan sixth chords* are found in Example Eleven, measure 17; Example Twelve, measure 3; Example Sixteen (Neapolitan in root position), measures 8 and 12; Example Seventeen, measure 12 (by enharmonic respelling); Example Twenty, measure 21.

2. *Augmented sixth chords* are found in Example Eight, measure 13; Example Nine, measures 7 and 25; Example Eleven, measure 26;

Example Twelve, measure 8; Example Thirteen, measure 8 (resolved irregularly); Example Sixteen, measures 6 and 10; Example Nineteen, measures 5, 7, and 9; Example Twenty, measures 2 and 6.

3. *Modal mixture* is found in Example Fourteen, measures 7 and 10; Example Fifteen, measure 21; Example Seventeen, measure 10.
4. *Augmented triads* are found in Example Nine, measures 1, 5, 17, and 19; Example Nineteen, measures 1, 5, 7, and 9.
5. *Chromatically altered pivot chords* are found in Example Eleven, measure 17 (bII$_6$) and measure 26 (Aug. sixth).

EXERCISES

1. In four parts, with a chord to precede the resolution, resolve N$_6$ to V in the following keys:

a minor	e minor
b minor	f minor
c minor	g minor
d minor	c sharp minor

2. Realize the following figured bass in four parts. Write in the Roman numerals first.

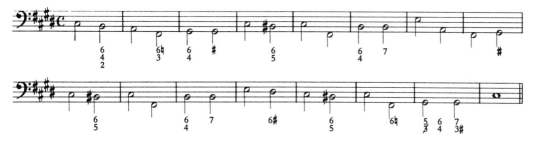

3. Make a four-part harmonization of the following soprano, using N$_6$ where marked *. Write in the Roman numeral analysis.

4. Harmonize the following soprano in four parts, using N₆ where appropriate. Write in the Roman numeral analysis.

5. In four parts, with a chord to precede the resolution, resolve each of the four kinds of augmented sixth chords in the following keys. If the resolution is to I_4^6, carry the resolution through the I_4^6 to V.

    F major   G major
    B flat major   D major
    E flat major   A major

6. Realize the following figured bass in four parts. Write in the Roman numerals first.

7. Harmonize the following soprano in four parts, using augmented sixth chords where marked ✶. Write in the Roman numeral analysis.

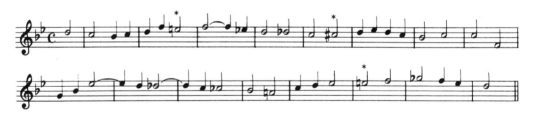

8. Harmonize the following soprano in four parts, using augmented sixth chords where appropriate. Write in the Roman numeral analysis.

9. Realize the following figured bass in four parts. Write in the Roman numerals first.

10. Harmonize the following in four parts, modulating as indicated. Use chromatically altered chords where altered tones suggest them and also as pivots where appropriate. (Any enharmonic respelling should be appropriate to the new key.)

11. Harmonize the following soprano in four parts; a mixture of modes is involved. Write in the Roman numeral analysis.

PART III

MUSICAL EXAMPLES FOR ANALYSIS

Overview

The short pieces and portions of longer works that appear in Part III serve two purposes: (1) to provide illustrations, in the context of the musical score, of the various harmonic principles and practices discussed in Part II; and (2) to provide a number of compositions that can be used by the student to develop analytical skills.

There is no aspect of musical study that does not require effective analytical skills. The purpose of analysis, even in a harmony course, is not merely to identify keys, chords and inversions, and nonharmonic tones. No single aspect of music can be profitably viewed without considering how the various musical elements interact with one another. Analysis becomes a fascinating study when one begins to gain insight into a composer's style and particular genius.

Before analyzing any of the music of Part III, one should become thoroughly familiar with the way the music sounds. One should play or listen to each piece again and again, until the music is clearly in mind. Each example was chosen because, among other things, it did not require a piano virtuoso to play it. As a point of beginning, one should consult the following section, "Analytic Projects," which attempts to point out specific questions that may lead to a better understanding of each of the examples. The next step is to look for important cadences and then for melodic repetition as a basic indicator of external musical form. After that, an analysis of the key areas, the chords and inversions, and the harmonic tones is appropriate. Harmonic analysis is only one of the aspects of analysis. Ideally, the analysis of each example should be as total as possible, utilizing all of the experience and information that can be brought to a consideration of the kind of statement each piece of music is making.

The more music one analyzes, the better one becomes at analysis. Analytical studies are like learning to become a detective. One gains a sensitivity to clues that can lead to exciting discoveries. Each musical composition based on the principles of harmony involves the utilization of similar concepts, but differing musical details. The discovery of how these varying means and proportions work together to establish the uniqueness of a given work is a moment of great reward.

Initially, one can scarcely expect to uncover musical subtleties through analysis. However, it is important always to realize that analysis will eventually lead to important musical discoveries. Since each piece is unique, it is not possible to generalize about the kinds of discoveries one might expect to find. However, it is exciting to discover such unities as the following example, taken from Bach's *Concerto for Two Violins in D Minor*, will show. The theme from the first movement involves the outline of a descending octave; it is interesting to note that the first themes from each of the other two movements also begin with the outline of a descending octave. At the very least, such a discovery shows one kind of unity that exists among the three movements.

Another kind of unity is shown in the following example, in which the melodic interval of the fourth is given great emphasis, both by leap and by scale progression.

J. S. Bach, WTC: Book I

In the following example, also by Bach, we see how a characteristic rhythmic motive, the thirty-second note figure, can provide both melodic and rhythmic unity.

J. S. Bach, Two-part Invention, No. 14

Finally, harmony students should realize that the farther one goes in the study of harmony, the more benefit can be derived from analysis. The first few examples in Part III have been chosen because of their simplicity, so that analysis can be started even though one may possess only a limited knowledge of harmony. Analysis plays an increasingly important role as each successive chapter is mastered.

The examples cover a span of time including the beginning of the eighteenth century and the middle of the nineteenth. While there is a somewhat chronological arrangement, the Strauss waltz from 1867 is placed as an early example because of its simplicity. Similarly, a minuet composed by Mozart in 1790 comes near the end of the examples because of its considerable chromatic activity. From this one can at least deduce that the passage of time in no way affects the complexity of a work.

LIST OF MUSICAL EXAMPLES[1]

---

1. The hymn by Vincent Novello, found on page 90 , provides another simple musical example for analysis projects.

ANALYTIC PROJECTS

Example One

1. Make a harmonic analysis (by Roman numerals).

2. Identify each cadence as to type.

3. The soprano melody contains repetitions of melodic ideas—mark these repetitions in the score.

Example Two

1. What soprano note is repeated most often in the first four measures? Would you deduce from this that the soprano (first four measures) is moving upward or downward, or is basically static?

2. What is the melodic direction of the soprano in the two measures following the double bar?

3. What is the basic melodic movement in the final phrase?

4. Which cadences are most like the others? Which cadence is least like the others?

Example Three

1. Reduce the sixteenth-note figuration of this piece into two five-part chords per measure (two half notes per measure, in block chords).

2. Encircle measures 7–11 and encircle measures 15–19. Notice that they are the same musical material, except that one is a fifth lower than the other.

3. In measure 6 the note F sharp is introduced, and no unaltered F is used in the passage that follows up to measure 13. What influence does the use of the F sharp have on the music between measures 6 and 11?

4. In measures 20 and 32 the note B flat is introduced. What influence does this B flat have on the music in those measures?

Example Four

1. Where does the modulation to G actually become effective? In other words, which F sharp is crucial in establishing the key of G major?

2. Why does the F sharp in measure 11 *not* establish the key of G?

3. Where is the crucial chromatic alteration that sets up the return from G major to C major?

4. Why does the introduction of the B flat in measure 8 *not* create a modulation to F major?

5. How many six-four chords can you find?

Example Five

1. Mark the cadence on B major and locate the chord containing the augmented sixth interval.

2. To what note does the A sharp resolve? To what note does the C resolve?

3. Why is the D natural so important in the first ending?

4. What factors keep a minor from being established at the first measure of the *Lebhaft*?

5. Why is the G natural so important in the second measure of the *Lebhaft*?

Example Six

1. What function does the F natural in measure 2 have?

2. Where does the D major restatement of the opening material actually begin? Draw lines on the score to connect the notes forming the descent of the perfect fourth from the D in the D major section (corresponding to the perfect fourth descent from the G in the first three measures).

3. Why does the C natural in the fifth measure *not* return the music to G major?

4. Where does the restatement of the music heard at the beginning actually occur in the final section?

5. What function does the C (natural) in measure 8 have?

Example Seven

1. Using the phrase symbols A', A'', B, and A'' (referred to in the paragraph introducing this example), mark the phrases of the musical score.

2. In what ways are A' and A'' similar? In what ways are they different?

3. In what ways is the B section similar to or different from the A sections?

4. How does Mozart keep the music from coming to a premature close three measures from the end?

5. Where is the melodic climax? How is it approached and how does the composer lead away from it?

Example Eight

1. Make a harmonic analysis of this example showing keys, chords, and inversions (Roman numerals).

2. The second section, which is in A flat, begins directly following a strong cadence in f minor. Has the composer prepared the music in any way to avoid an abrupt sound when it moves to A flat?

3. Mark the resolutions of the notes forming the augmented sixth chord in measure 13. Which kind of augmented sixth chord is it?

4. What similarities exist between the last four measures and the first eight measures?

Example Nine

1. Make a piano version of this example by placing the first and second violin parts on the treble staff, and the viola and cello parts on the bass staff. Try to retain the voice leading exactly as Haydn has written it.

2. Mark all diminished seventh chords and augmented sixth chords.

3. Mark all phrases and analyze each cadence according to key and Roman numerals.

4. Identify pivot chords where a change of key has occurred.

Example Ten

1. Using the symbols A, B, A', mark the score to show repetition structure. How do the last four measures relate to this scheme? Do you need another symbol for that last phrase?

2. Make a harmonic analysis, showing keys, chords, and inversions (Roman numerals).

3. Discuss the similarities and differences that exist between the B section and the A section.

4. Discuss the similarities and differences that exist between the last four measures and the rest of the piece.

Example Eleven

1. In this example there are several building blocks. One is the triplet figure (in the right hand) that moves from the C up to the F; this is then followed by a cadence on c minor in measure 5. Then the process repeats itself in lower octaves. In measure 7 this figure is used for a long scalewise ascent. How far up does this ascent go before it cadences again on C? Mark lines on the score to connect the notes involved in the ascent.

2. Another building block is the figure involving a quarter note followed by four sixteenth notes, effecting a motivic descent of a fourth, leading to a Neapolitan sixth chord. Write in the appropriate Roman numeral for the N_6, and then identify its other function as a pivot chord in the new key.

3. The last eight measures present a new theme in A flat major. Locate the pivot chord that facilitates the return to c minor and write in the Roman numerals for that pivot, appropriate to both the old and the new keys.

Example Twelve

1. Locate and identify (by Roman numerals) all chromatically altered chords (diminished seventh, Neapolitan sixth, and augmented sixth).

2. Locate and identify (by Roman numeral) the pivot chord that effects the modulation from e minor to D major.

3. How many irregular resolutions of dominants or secondary dominants can you find?

Example Thirteen

1. How do you explain the resolution of the augmented sixth chord in measure 8? To what would you normally expect it to resolve?

2. What is the key in measures 9 and 10? Where and how does the music return to a minor?

3. Locate and identify all diminished seventh chords.

Example Fourteen

1. Has the piece modulated to the dominant when it has made a cadence on C? Or do you think it has made a cadence on V, preceded by secondary dominants? Give reasons for making your choice.

2. The first few measures present important melodic material; that musical idea recurs several times throughout the piece. Mark each occurrence.

3. Locate and identify all key areas you feel are established in the piece.

4. Locate and identify (by Roman numerals) all pivot chords in the piece.

5. Is there a climax in the piece? Give reasons to support your decision if you do locate a climax.

Example Fifteen

1. Using the symbols A, A', B, mark the score to show the repetition structure of this short piece. If there are additional features that deserve additional identification, devise an appropriate symbol or verbal caption for those features. How do you identify the last five measures? How do you identify measures 7 and 8?

2. Where is a variation technique employed?

3. Make a Roman numeral analysis of measures 13–16. Be sure to show exactly where the Roman numeral identification should be changed to conform to Schumann's spelling of the chords.

4. What Roman numeral analysis is most appropriate for the *più p* chord five measures from the end?

5. Where do you feel the climax of the piece comes? Give reasons to support your decision.

Example Sixteen

1. In the second measure a progression in A flat major is clearly presented, and in the fourth measure a progression in G major is clearly presented. What factors prevent these measures from being heard as modulations away from c minor?

2. Assuming that the symbol A can represent the first four measures and that the symbol B can represent measures 5–8 and 9–12, discuss all possible similarities and differences between A and B.

3. Locate the Neapolitan chords and the augmented sixth chords, and take note of their resolution. How do you explain the fourth chord of measures 5 and 9?

4. Is there a climax? If so, where? Give reasons.

Example Seventeen

1. Appoggiaturas are an important feature of this famous melody. How many does this excerpt contain and where are they?

2. Measures 5–8 are an elaborated statement of the material presented in the first four measures. What differences actually exist between the two passages?

3. Make a harmonic analysis (Roman numerals) giving particular attention to the last two measures. Assume that the key throughout is E flat major.

Example Eighteen

1. The first seven eighth notes in the uppermost part (played by the right hand) are a most important motive. How many restatements of that motive can you find in the vocal parts or the instrumental accompaniment? Where does it occur in augmentation?

2. Where does a mixture of modes (minor in major context) occur? Where, and by what means, does the music modulate to D major?

Example Nineteen

1. Mark the section that is clearly in D major and mark the section that is clearly in A major. Between those two key areas are three sequential patterns; put brackets around them and then decide what the tonal emphasis of each pattern is.

2. Mark (with Roman numerals) each augmented triad and each augmented sixth chord.

3. Where is the climax of the piece? Why do you feel it is the climax? What purpose do the dynamic markings serve?

Example Twenty

1. Make a harmonic analysis of the first phrase, thinking of it (for simplicity) as a progression in a minor.

2. Make a harmonic analysis of the second phrase, thinking of it in C major. Then make a harmonic analysis of the third phrase, thinking of it in E major.

3. Continue analyzing from this point, going as far as you can in the key of C major. Note the use of Neapolitan sixth in measure 21.

4. Note the similarity between the material of measures 18–21 and 33–36.

5. Note the use of sequential material at the beginning and at measures 25–32.

EXAMPLE ONE

"Old Hundredth" (Psalm 134, "Or sus, serviteurs du Seigneur"). Melody from the Genevan Psalter, 1551.

This familiar melody, possibly composed by Louis Bourgeois, has appeared with many different harmonizations over the years. The setting presented here was chosen because of its suitability as a beginning exercise in harmonic analysis. No significance with respect to the evolution of music should be inferred, even though this piece is the earliest of the examples presented in this section. It was chosen because it is made up primarily of triads in root position, and the harmonization contains almost no altered tones.[1] Moreover, this harmonization offers a clear illustration of various kinds of cadences (the final chord of each phrase is marked by a fermata sign). The first is a perfect authentic cadence; the second, a half cadence; the third, deceptive; and the final one, a perfect authentic cadence. The key is clearly G major throughout, with completely diatonic harmonies. The highest soprano note is D, and this is a melodic climax that has been well placed, just at the beginning of the final phrase.

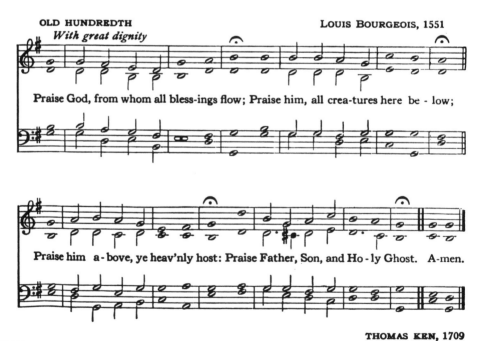

OLD HUNDREDTH   LOUIS BOURGEOIS, 1551
With great dignity

Praise God, from whom all bless-ings flow; Praise him, all crea-tures here be - low;

Praise him a - bove, ye heav'nly host: Praise Father, Son, and Ho - ly Ghost. A-men.

THOMAS KEN, 1709

"Old Hundredth" by Louis Bourgeois and "Albano" by Vincent Novello. Reprinted from *The Hymnal of the Protestant Episcopal Church, 1940*, prepared by the Joint Commission on the Hymnal. Copyright 1940 by the Church Pension Fund, N.Y.

1. With the exception of the C sharp three measures from the end (a dominant function borrowed from D major). An extensive discussion of this type of procedure will be found in Chapter 15.

EXAMPLE TWO

"Du Friedensfürst, Herr Jesu Christ." Chorale from Cantata 67, "Halt' im Gedächtnis Jesum Christ," by J. S. Bach. Composed between 1723 and 1727.

This melody has been given various musical settings by Bach in three different cantatas. The version here is particularly suited to analysis by beginning students in harmony because of its few nonharmonic tones and because of the relative absence of chromatic alterations. There are comparatively more root-position triads than the excellent bass line would lead one to expect, although there are several inverted triads (a passing six-four in the next-to-last measure is also present). The single chromatic alteration (E sharp) is the leading tone in the scale of f sharp minor (the chord involved is the dominant of that key), and this leading tone participates in a point of harmonic intensity or climax just before the final phrase. The repetition structure of the piece may be charted as follows:

$$\|:A'\ A'':\|B\ A'''\|$$

(A′‴ contains elements of both of the first two phrases, as though the two phrases were compressed into one.)

Du Friedensfürst, Herr Jesu Christ *

"Du Friedensfurst, Herr Jesu Christ," Number 42 from *Bach Riemenschneider, 371 Harmonized Chorales* edited by Albert Riemenschneider. Copyright 1941 by G. Schirmer. Used by permission of the publisher.

EXAMPLE THREE

Prelude in C, from Well-tempered Clavier, *Book I, by J. S. Bach. Composed in 1722.*

This is the first prelude in the series of forty-eight (two series of twenty-four) preludes and fugues that Bach wrote exploring every major and minor key. The fact that each note of this keyboard piece sounds out alone does not alter the actual conception of the piece in terms of five individual melodic voices. The chords change measure by measure, and the five separate parts are articulated and implied by means of chord arpeggiation. Note the frequent use of the nondominant seventh, formed as the seventh is added as a suspended dissonant note. The most important division of the piece occurs with the authentic cadence progression in measures 18 and 19. In the section following that point, and particularly in the final measures, there is a subdominant emphasis that is characteristic of a great many pieces by Bach. Note that measures 7 to 11 reappear in transposed form in measures 15 to 19.

"Das Wohltemperirte Clavier Erster Theil, Preludium 1" by J.S. Bach. Reprinted from *Bach: Werke,* Edition Bach-Geselschaft. Published by Breitkopf and Härtel.

EXAMPLE FOUR

"Pastoral Symphony," from Messiah, *by G. F. Handel. Composed in 1741.*

This gentle movement for string orchestra, composed in the characteristic manner of pastorales (written in 12/8 meter and employing droning pedal notes in the bass), provides an example of the use of pedal tones. The pedal tones here are prolonged tonic or dominant notes, and as can be expected their use results in a static harmonic character. The piece emphasizes the key of C for the first eleven measures and also for the last eleven measures (which are, of course, an exact musical restatement). The middle third of the piece (measures 12 to 21) shows an emphasis of G first as the dominant of C, and then, through a subtle modulation, as a tonic in its own right. The middle section is introduced by the bass in measure 12 with the same ascending scale melody that occurs in the first measure; similarly, the bass in measure 21 uses this motive as a means of introducing the return to C and the restatement of the material of the first section. Note the consistent use of the cadential six-four chord.

Movement 13 PIFA (Pastoral Symphony), measures 1–21 from *Messiah* by G.F. Handel edited by J.M. Coopersmith copyright 1947 by Carl Fischer Inc. N.Y. Reprinted by permission.

EXAMPLE FIVE

Third Waltz, from "An der schönen blauen Donau" ("Blue Danube"), by Johann Strauss. Composed in 1867.

This example is not presented in chronological order with the other examples in this section and is not intended to demonstrate a particular development of harmonic style. It is presented at this point because of its rather simple harmonic structure and because it provides a useful demonstration of the use of nonharmonic tones. The harmonic style is simple because of the lighter character of the music, a popular Viennese dance style of the nineteenth century. Strauss was the acknowledged master of the idiom. In spite of the simple harmonic structure, an augmented sixth chord does occur in measure 14, in the approach to a Phrygian cadence on B major. No modulation actually occurs, and this is underscored by the fact that the music immediately proceeds (from that cadence) in the key of G major. The harmonic rhythm of the opening section is quite slow, with the tonic chord being retained for the first six measures. After this, four measures of dominant harmony are heard. Following the double bar, the harmonic rhythm changes more predictably, measure by measure.

"On the Beautiful Blue Danube," Third Waltz, measures 1–35 and First Waltz, measures 1–16 by J. Strauss from *59 Piano Solos You Like to Play*. Copyright 1936 by G. Schirmer.

EXAMPLE SIX

Introduction to Duet (7th movement), Cantata no. 15, "Denn du wirst meine Seele nicht in der Hölle lassen." This is an early eighteenth-century work attributed (probably spuriously) to J. S. Bach.

This piano reduction of the original instrumental score clearly divides into three sections. The first section is in G major. The second section is nearly a literal restatement of the first, but this time in the dominant (D major). The final section is a restatement of the opening, concluded by a more emphatic cadence than was used to end the first section. The form is clearly A B A. Of particular interest is the treatment of the leading tone (F sharp) at the end of the first measure, which resolves down in a harmonic sequence to F natural. The same circumstance occurs again in measure 9. This chromatic movement facilitates a melodic descent of a perfect fourth from G to D. Between measures 4 and 5 the C sharp to C natural functions in the same manner in the key of D major, where the melodic descent of the perfect fourth occurs in an inner voice. The cadence in measure 4 is bridged by eliding the conclusion of the G major section with the beginning of the D major section. A more emphatic division occurs in measure 8, where the D major section concludes before the restatement of the opening G major material.

"Now with Rejoicing and Laughter" by J.S. Bach reprinted with the permission of the publisher E.C. Schirmer Music Co., Boston. Available in a collection entitled *48 Duets*, edited by Victor Prahl.

EXAMPLE SEVEN

First Movement (beginning), Sonata in A, K. 331, by W. A. Mozart. Composed in 1778.

This famous theme, opening the variations movement that in a rather unusual placement begins the sonata, is laid out in clear and regular phrases as follows:

$$\|{:}A'\ A''{:}\|\ \|{:}B\ A''\ \text{cad.}{:}\|$$

The harmonic scheme is simple (using only a single accidental), and the key remains unchanged throughout. The B section places emphasis on the subdominant. A continuous pedal tone on the dominant is to be found in the middle voice of the A section, and it drops out for an instant only at the *sforzando* first-inversion supertonic chord in the approach to the cadence. Similarly, there is within the B section a persistent tonic note in the bass. The use of appoggiatura six-four chords provides stylistic unity among the cadences. The dependence of outer voices on each other should be noted in the A section, where they form a duet at the interval of a tenth.

"Sonata" K. 331, First Movement, measures 1–18 from *Mozart's Sonatas and Fantasies for the Piano*, edited by Nathan Broder. Copyright © 1956 by Theodore Presser Co. Used by permission of the publisher.

EXAMPLE EIGHT

Second Movement (exposition), Sonata in F, K. 280, by W. A. Mozart, Composed in 1774.

The sonata from which this excerpt is taken, based on a model of Haydn, speaks strongly in that composer's terms. A particularly striking feature of this example is the use of sharply contrasted dynamics, a result in part of the growing interest in the development of the pianoforte (with its greater dynamic range) as opposed to the harpsichord. This movement opens with an f minor triad that is followed immediately by the dominant of the relative major. However, the latter chord is resolved irregularly into the dominant of f minor, which in turn resolves deceptively to the submediant (over which is placed a dissonant double appoggiatura). This rich harmonic scheme is finally closed by an authentic cadence in f minor. The remainder of the example is in A flat major, which was actually forecast in the second measure of this example. The augmented sixth chord in measure 13 is made to function more specifically as a dominant of the dominant when the F flat of measure 13 is replaced by an F natural in measure 15.

"Sonata in F," K.280 by W.A. Mozart, Second Movement, measures 1–24. Reprinted from *W.A. Mozart Clavier Sonaten,* Band 1 edited by Walther Lampe. Copyright © 1977 G. Henle Verlag, Munich. Used by permission.

EXAMPLE NINE

Second Movement (theme), Quartet in F, op. 74, no. 2, by F. J. Haydn, Composed in 1793.

This deceptively simple example shows a harmonic inventiveness that includes augmented sixth chords (measures 7 and 25), several diminished seventh chords (measures 6, 12, 13 and 24), and secondary dominants. There is a rather unique use of an upward resolving appoggiatura in the viola part (G sharp in the first measure) that gives rise to an augmented triad in second inversion. This, of course, returns with subsequent repetitions of that material (measures 5, 17, and 19). The first few notes of the principal theme form a melodic and rhythmic motive that is exploited subsequently in sequence and by inversion. A characteristic unifying factor is the dominant-over-tonic appoggiatura in each cadence.

Second Movement, measures 1–26 from *Haydn Quartet, Opus 74, number 2, in F Major* edited by Wilhelm Altman. Used by permission of European American Music Distributors Corporation, sole U.S. Agent for Ernst Eulenberg Ltd.

EXAMPLE TEN

Second Movement (theme), Sonata in G, op. 14, no. 2, by L. van Beethoven. Published in 1799.

This portion of the second movement of an early sonata by Beethoven provides the formal unity and completeness of a short piece. The use of secondary dominants throughout is of particular interest, and these are especially forceful in the sequential passage in measures 17 and 18 (where they are underscored with offbeat *sforzando* markings), leading into the final cadence. There are three occasions in which diminished seventh chords are used as secondary dominants; however, it should be noted that the chord on the second beat of measure 7 might have been spelled contrapuntally more correctly with an A sharp instead of a B flat (in fact, Beethoven does use the A sharp spelling in a subsequent variation). From a standpoint of unity and diversity, it is interesting to note the contrast that is presented in the four measures following the double bar, providing the only subdominant emphasis and departing at the same time from the energetic staccato that is so characteristic of the rest of the piece.

"Sonata" Opus 14, number 2, Second Movement measures 1–20 and "Sonata" Opus 13 (Pathetique), measures 182–210 by L. van Beethoven. Reprinted from *L. van Beethoven Werke*. Published by Breitkopf and Härtel.

EXAMPLE ELEVEN

*Coda from the Finale, Sonata in C Minor, op. 13 (*Pathétique*), by L. van Beethoven. Published in 1799.*

This portion of the movement, the conclusion of the last movement of a lengthy sonata in c minor, presents the strongest possible confirmation of that key. It begins with an emphasis of the subdominant that leads into an emphatic cadence progression in measures 4 and 5. This is followed by a repetition of the subdominant emphasis, which this second time leads into an expanded presentation of the triplet figure, ascending in the right hand by scalewise steps, measure by measure, to the note D. From this point, the melodic line returns to B natural and finally settles on a C cadence. Tonal emphasis in this section is achieved by cadential harmonic progression, by frequent reiteration of the note C (left hand, measures 1–3 and 5–7; right hand, measures 1–10), and by steady lineal ascent from middle C to the C above (right hand, measure 17   ). A cadence theme is then introduced that modulates in measures 17 to A flat major by means of a pivot chord that is Neapolitan sixth in c minor and IV_6 in A flat. After a prolonged descent on the dominant seventh of A flat, a fragment of the main theme of the movement is presented. This leads into a sudden return to c minor through the ambiguity of the augmented sixth chord of C (which was V_7 of IV in A flat). Of course, this brief modulation is really only prolonged emphasis of the submediant of c minor and as a result does not confuse the emphasis of key in the approach to a final cadence.

"Sonata" Opus 14, number 2, Second Movement measures 1–20 and "Sonata" Opus 13 (Pathetique), measures 182–210 by L. van Beethoven. Reprinted from *L. van Beethoven Werke*. Published by Breitkopf and Härtel.

EXAMPLE TWELVE

Agnus Dei (first Agnus only), from Mass in G, *by F. Schubert. Composed in 1815.*

This example is a piano reduction of the original score (involving string orchestra and organ accompaniment). One of the more interesting harmonic features is the use of the Neapolitan sixth chord as the chord of resolution in the deceptive cadence of measure 3. Other chromatically altered chords include diminished sevenths (in measures 3 and 4) and an augmented sixth chord at the beginning of measure 8. Note the modulation, via pivot chord and mixture of major and minor modes, that occurs in measure 8. The rhythm, dynamics, and chromatic lineal movement (opposite motion between outer voices) of this passage all combine to give strong support to the tonal change effected by the somewhat abrupt irregular resolution of V_7 of F (V_7 of D). The use of numerous appoggiaturas throughout the example, resolving upward as well as downward, serves to provide an additional unification through the use of nonharmonic tones.

"Mass in G" by Franz Schubert "Agnus Dei" measures 1–14 reprinted from *Messe von Franz Schubert*, edition 5754 published by C.F. Peters, Leipzig.

EXAMPLE THIRTEEN

Capriccio in A, op. 16, no. 1 (beginning), by F. Mendelssohn. Composed in 1831.

This example begins quietly and simply, using two voices for the greater portion of the first four measures to imply the harmonies involved. The texture thickens after measure 5 with the free addition of voices until the long diminished seventh chord arpeggios in measures 15 and 17. It is interesting to note the emphasis achieved by the sudden *pianissimo* dynamic marking that is placed on the unusual resolution of the augmented sixth chord in measure 8. This progression serves to turn the tonality temporarily toward the relative major. The harmonic scheme is otherwise quite simple, making little use of secondary dominants other than V_7 of IV. Nonharmonic tones such as passing tones and appoggiaturas often occur doubly in parallel thirds.

"Capriccio in A," opus 16 number 1 by F. Mendelssohn, measures 1–20 from *Sonatina Album for the Piano.*
Copyright 1893 by G. Schirmer.

EXAMPLE FOURTEEN

"Träumerei," from Kinderscenen, op. 15, by R. Schumann. Composed in 1838.

This short piece is harmonically quite complicated because of its modulations and the modal mixtures it uses. In measure 7 we find an f minor chord in an F major context, and in measure 10 we find a c minor chord in an F major context. Observe the contrapuntal use to which these chords are put. In addition to secondary dominants and diminished seventh chords, there is a complete minor ninth chord at the climax in measure 14 and a complete major ninth chord at the final moment of climax three measures from the end. The opening melodic idea assumes an important role, appearing several times in the home key, but also briefly and emphatically in B flat major. The analysis of this short work provides a lesson in modulation, moving from F major to a cadence on the dominant, returning to F major, then moving quickly to B flat major after a cadence on g minor. The music then moves with finesse through a cadence in d minor back to the home key for the final eight measures.

"Träumerei" and "Der Dichter Spricht," Number 13 reprinted from Schuman Kinderscenen, Opus 15. Edition 8278 published by C.F. Peters, Leipzig.

EXAMPLE FIFTEEN

"Der Dichter spricht," from Kinderscenen, *op. 15, by Robert Schumann. Composed in 1838.*

This short piece is the final one of a series of thirteen such compositions. It is interesting to note the variation of the first phrase that occurs in measure 9, providing at once a sense of unity, progress, and even contrast, all the while making use of the same basic harmonic and melodic material. These varied phrases are interrupted midway, setting the scene for the much greater contrast that is to follow in the more rhapsodic, cadenza-like passage. After the carefully measured and reasonably predictable rhythmic, melodic, and harmonic character of the first section, the rhythmic freedom, the vertical melodic contour, and the harmonic ambiguity of the diminished seventh chord arpeggiation come more as a flight of fancy than a new thematic idea. Note the enharmonic change of spelling in the descending diminished seventh chord arpeggio, which gives a visual, but not an aural appearance of change. The final measures are an extension of the cadence in a minor that occurred in measures 8 and 21.

"Träumerei" and "Der Dichter Spricht," Number 13 reprinted from Schuman Kinderscenen, Opus 15. Edition 8278 published by C.F. Peters, Leipzig.

EXAMPLE SIXTEEN

Prelude in C Minor, op. 28, no. 20, by F. Chopin. One of twenty-four preludes composed by Chopin between 1836 and 1839.

This short and relatively simple work begins with an opening statement of four measures. Without repeating the first statement, the second idea emerges in measures 5–8. The second idea, rather than the first, is then repeated. Although the work is clearly in c minor, the second measure restates the material of the first measure literally in A flat major, the submediant of c minor. The third measure returns to c minor, but the fourth measure provides a strong cadence on G major, the dominant of c minor. The emphasis in the first four measures is c minor, A flat major, c minor, G major—all placed over a strong bass that has very little stepwise movement. In measure 5 and what follows, the bass engages in a lineal descent from C to E flat, cadencing again with the strong leaps that characterized the bass of the first four measures. All of the cadences in the piece involve feminine endings, and the final cadence is strengthened by the repetition of the c minor chord, a quiet exclamation point to conclude the piece. Harmonically interesting is the chord on the second beat of measures 6 and 10—it is a French augmented sixth chord. There is also a Neapolitan chord in root position in measures 8 and 12, and this is the same chord that was introduced on the second beat of the second measure, in an ambiguous context of A flat major.

"Prelude" Number 20, Brown-Index 107, reprinted from *Chopin Préludes,* edited by E. Zimmerman. Copyright © 1969 G. Henle Verlag, Munich. Used by permission.

EXAMPLE SEVENTEEN

Nocturne, op. 9, no. 2 (beginning), by F. Chopin. Composed in 1831.

This piece involves a pianistic style consisting of a single, flowing melody with a chordal accompaniment. One is scarcely aware of the importance of voice leading at first glance, because the accompaniment appears simply to employ chord spacings that are merely a result of the particular hand position desired. A more careful investigation reveals the most sensitive awareness of contrapuntal resolution by Chopin. Measures 5 through 8 are a melodic elaboration of the first four measures. Measure 9 seems to present a new section emphasizing the area of the dominant key, but the subdominant chord (first in the major mode and then in the minor form) in measure 10 immediately reinstates the key of E flat major. Following this, the key is again stretched toward dominant regions, only to return to E flat in measure 13 (theme var.) through a rapid and rich succession of chords in measure 12. Note the E major triad in measure 12, which can, by enharmonic respelling, be seen to be Neapolitan sixth in E flat, preceded by its own dominant (of course, V_7 of N_6 is enharmonically identical to the augmented sixth in the same key).

"Nocturne," Opus 9, number 2 by F. Chopin, measures 1–13 reprinted from *Chopin Album for the Piano: Schirmer's Library of Music Classics,* Volume 39, edited by Rafael Joseffy. Copyright 1915 by G. Schirmer.

EXAMPLE EIGHTEEN

"Ir habt nun Traurigkeit" (beginning), from Ein deutsches Requiem, *by J. Brahms. Composed in 1868.*

This example, a piano reduction of a work scored for orchestral accompaniment, begins clearly in G major and does not depart significantly from this area until measure 19. Key feeling in this section is established primarily through prolongation and emphasis of the dominant. Within the first three measure introduction, the dominant chord is placed on the accented beats and is given cadential emphasis. From measure 4 to the upbeat of measure 17, there is no tonic chord at all. However, D as a dominant is prolonged throughout that section, with digression only in measures 6 and 7, where the subdominant is emphasized; or in measures 12 and 13, where D minor is indicated; or where cadences on the dominant are preceded by V of V. At measure 18, the material of the beginning returns again briefly, but the cadence on D this time functions as a modulation to D major. A new harmonic color is added by the brief implication of b minor in measures 21 and 22, and again in measures 24 and 25. The use of phrases of varying and irregular lengths, and the use of such contrapuntal devices as the melodic augmentation of the principal instrumental melody in the section beginning in D major should also be noted.

Movement 5, measures 1–26 reprinted from *Ein Deutches Requiem,* Opus 45 by J. Brahms Edition 6071 published by Breitkopf and Härtel, Weisbaden.

EXAMPLE NINETEEN

Minuet, K. 335 (594a) (beginning), by W. A. Mozart. Composed in 1790.

This minuet, for which Mozart did not compose a trio, was published in the year 1801 in conjunction with a trio that had been composed by M. Stadler. This example is not presented in chronological order among the examples because it shows a remarkably chromatic texture. Its chromaticism arises out of sequential patterns that, because of double groupings of accidentals in lineal movement from an augmented triad through an augmented sixth chord, relate somewhat to the following Wagner example (Example Twenty). The augmented triad occurs frequently (measures 1, 5, 7, 9), as does the augmented sixth chord (measures 5, 7, 9). The sequential pattern is introduced with stepwise preparation (measures 5 and 6) and is restated with stepwise preparation (measures 7 and 8); however, the third statement (measures 9 and 10) is introduced without such preparation, and yet it is musically logical because of the strength of the pattern itself. Mozart uses the *forte* dynamic marking four times, and three of these times underscore the sequential pattern beginning. The first four measures are clearly in D major; the first sequential pattern begins with root movement around the circle of fifths (C sharp–F sharp–B), and this is continued in the second statement of the pattern (B–E–A). The final pattern restates the roots E and A, moving to D as a subdominant, preparing the key of A major, which is heard in the last six measures.

"Minuet" K.335(594a) by W.A. Mozart, measures 1–19 reprinted from *More Classics to Moderns* edited by Denes Agay. Copyright © 1960 by Consolidated Music, a division of Music Sales Corp., N.Y. Used by permission of the publisher.

EXAMPLE TWENTY

Prelude to Tristan und Isolde *(beginning), by R. Wagner. Composed in 1859.*

This famous example is one of the most difficult compositions to analyze in all of tonal music. By means of sequences, by means of double and triple groupings of chromatic nonharmonic tones, by means of chromatic lineal movement, the concept of tonality is expanded to an extremely broad perspective. The tonality, constantly shifting by means of unique chromatic alteration, by the process of sequential restatement, or by the use of long scalewise chains of altered tones, develops a transitory and often ambiguous character. Of particular interest here is the resolution of the augmented sixth chord (in measure 2) to V_7 of a minor in measure 3; the same progression is sequentially restated up a minor third (enharmonic respelling is partly involved) to provide the resolution of augmented sixth to V_7 of C; then a third and somewhat similar statement (this time omitting what had in the earlier patterns been the upper note of the augmented sixth interval) ends on V_7 of E. This last statement is echoed an octave higher, followed by a reechoing of the notes E sharp and F sharp that provide the impetus for a new, more lyrical melody that has considerable C emphasis as it wends its chromatic way through conventional and unconventional processes (note the Neapolitan sixth of D in measure 21) toward the cadential pause on an A major triad. Midstream restatements of earlier material lead to a varied restatement of the lyrical melody, again emphasizing C, as all approaches to cadential repose vanish into thin air and unpredicted tonal emphases.

Measures 1–37 reprinted from *Tristan and Isolde* by R. Wagner. Copyright 1906 by G. Schirmer.

Index